The Bicycle Repair Shop

A True Story of Recovery from
Multiple Personality Disorder

As Told by Patient and Therapist

Angela Fisher & Todd E. Pressman, Ph.D.

"There are no bicycles beyond repair"

To the reader:

At certain points in this narrative, names and other identifying information have been changed to protect anonymity and confidentiality. In no way did this affect the content of the story.

Table Of Contents

Table Of Contents 4

Prologue 6

Preface 9

Introduction-The Therapeutic Background 12

Chapter 1-Angela's Story 21

Chapter 2-The Personalities Come Forth 32

Chapter 3-Angie And The Boss 43

Chapter 4-The Little Ones And Patrick 48

Chapter 5-Healing Crisis 59

Chapter 6-"All This Is My Fault" 69

Chapter 7-The First Splitting 73

Chapter 8-Growing Up 78

Chapter 9-Angie's Birth, Life And Death 86

Chapter 10-The Therapeutic Transference 94

Chapter 11-The Marriage Years 99

Chapter 12-Mother 103

Chapter 13-My Anger Starts To Come Out 109

Chapter 14-Building Strength And Courage 117

Chapter 15-Getting At The Source Of My Anger 122

Chapter 16-Wanting To Kill My Father 131

Chapter 17-Spiritual Journeys 137

Chapter 18-Michael 144

Chapter 19-Pulling Out Another Memory................... 161

Chapter 20-Tang... 169

Chapter 21-Shark...173

Chapter 22-Forgiving My Father And Mother................187

Chapter 23-Taking Stock Of My Life 192

Chapter 24-Integration: A Whole New Meaning 197

Chapter 26-Letting Love In And Out......................... 203

Epilogue..,207

In Appreciation...214

Appendix..216

Healing..217

Bibliography..222

Biography-Todd Pressman..227

Biography-Angela Fisher...229

Prologue

Dream sequence:

I find myself in a large factory with ceilings at least 20 feet high. Great ramps go up and down on each side of the room, from the floor to halfway up the walls. Around the top of the factory are two doors which remain closed. There are pictures painted on the walls and it is very bright and cheery. On the floor are hundreds of bikes in need of repair. In the center of the building is a large spiral escalator. It is so high that no one can see the top. I could only see from the floor to the first landing. The escalator is beautiful. It fills almost the whole room and is covered at the very bottom with green lush carpet. The carpet changes color somewhere in the middle. It goes from green to orange and then a magnificent red. Bikes hang from the escalator and are being raised slowly as they go around the spiral. The bikes which are hanging are the ones that are repaired. The bikes on the floor are the ones in need of repair. There are a lot of people arriving with their bikes. Most of them are dragging or carrying their bikes since they are unable to ride them. I felt that I was only a voice and could see anywhere I wanted. A young man with dark hair was busy as a bee repairing the bikes. He looked up, smiled and welcomed me into his factory.

Todd: Can I help you?
Voice: Todd, are you going to fix all of these bikes?
Todd: Any bike that is brought to me will be fixed.
Voice: Some of them look beyond repair.
Todd: There is no bike that is beyond repair.

At this point I noticed that there were bike parts all over the floor. Todd had a basket and was picking up all of the parts that he needed.

Voice: I have a bike that needs repair but I don't think you can fix it. There are parts missing and I don't know where they are.
Todd: If you bring the bike to me, I will fix it.
Voice: I don't believe that you could fix all bikes. There has to have been at least one that you were unable to fix. How can you say that with such confidence?
Todd: I am sure I can find the parts that are missing. Will you give me your bike?

I looked around Todd's wonderful factory and said, "Here it is".

Like magic, next to Todd was my bike that looked like it was run over by a truck. It was hard to tell it was ever a bike except for the front.

Todd: Oh! I can fix that.

Shortly after, a very young girl entered the room. She walked up to Todd with her bike and said, "Would you look at my bike and see if it is in need of repair?" Todd took the bike, turned it upside down, spinning the wheels, and then said, "Your bike does not need repair at this time, but in a few

7

years when the bike is older, it will probably be in need of some repairs". The young girl took her bike back feeling good that is was not broken, but also felt sad knowing that at sometime it would be in need of repair. Todd, noticing the sadness in her face said, "Bikes are made to break; it is the only way they are brought for repair". The young girl walked over to Todd, looked up at him, and said, "I have a dream that someday God will make bikes that never need repair". Todd then put his arm around her and answered, "I have the same dream".

I knew that my bike, like all the others, would be repaired. As Todd said, "There is no bike which is beyond repair".

Preface

This is the remarkable true story of one women's recovery from Multiple Personality Disorder. Her name is Angela Fisher. Multiple Personality Disorder, commonly called MPD, has the technical name of Dissociative Identity Disorder. This name suggests a condition where one dissociates or "splits off" into various personalities for the purpose of managing otherwise unbearable circumstances. In MPD, when things become too difficult, the primary personality "takes leave" of reality and goes into a sort of hiding place, tuning out and turning off their awareness of the situation. Another personality, sometimes called an "alter", then emerges, one whose characteristics make them better equipped to deal with the situation. Often, a staggering array of personalities can come forth at different times, according to which will best serve the needs of the moment. [1]

---

[1] There is some debate about the validity of Multiple Personality Disorder (or DID) as a diagnosis, and of repressed memories in general. The argument goes that MPD is a socially constructed idea that the patient buys into and that repressed memories are merely the product of an interpretation the therapist imposes. I will not engage this debate here but merely say it is a therapist's highest responsibility to listen to and respect a patient's experience, even if not based on fact. Of course, the therapist must prevent the patient from taking any action which may impact another, until such facts become certain. Beyond this, it is the therapist's sacred task to help the patient feel understood and neither deny their experience or impose their view. The patient, on the other hand, has the responsibility of never buying the therapist's view until they can honestly make it their own. If a therapeutic interpretation is true, it will bear fruit; insights will follow, remembrances of the past that make sense out of the interpretation will spontaneously occur and healing will result. If an interpretation is untrue, it will quickly and powerfully bump up against the patient's natural self-protection (which must be distinguished from initial resistance) and fall flat. The therapist need only suggest and offer ideas, giving reflective feedback as appropriate, and follow the signs of truth along the way.

While the particular diagnosis of MPD provides the backdrop for this story, it is intended to offer a much wider message. For MPD is just one of the ways we all "dissociate", splitting off from parts of ourselves and aspects of reality to deal with what feels too awful to bear. Not that most of us become oblivious to our basic personality or immediate surroundings. But when we find ourselves responding to the world with our usual habits and defensive postures, we do indeed disown parts of our identity--who we really are. These parts of ourselves must in the end be brought back into full awareness; a process called "integration". The ultimate goal of healing is to positively embrace the whole of ourselves and the whole of our lives in courageous acceptance. As Angela's story shows, this is the key that spontaneously opens the door to a higher meaning, transforming our struggles into a profound sense of purpose and fulfillment, regardless of our circumstances.

Therefore, while this book describes Angela's path to healing through her psychotherapy, it is also intended to show that whenever therapist and patient come together in a spirit of true commitment, they can open the way from fear and fragmentation to peace and wholeness. It is my hope that we may each find ourselves in this one woman's saga and understand our own journey, that we may see Angela's story of recovery as our shared story. Even though the circumstances of her past and her healing were unique, they are but an example of the one path we are all on. For each of us is caught in the same web of pain and confusion, having separated from the love we need, building up walls of protection against it. Angela's story is, therefore, a piece of the script we continue to write by the living of our lives. It is the story of our daily struggle and our lifetime's evolution, the movement from separation to oneness, from fearful defensiveness to wholeness and unity. Her story and the map for change it lays out take us past the limits of where psychotherapy too often stops--the healing of the individual--to point the way to therapy's true potential--our healing as a humanity. For in the integration of who we really are, we must understand our place in a greater picture, serving not only our individual wishes, but the nobler purpose for which this miraculous thing called life was created.

Introduction :

The Therapeutic Background

I remember well the first time I met Angela, some 6 years ago. It was at a group meeting I was conducting on *A Course in Miracles*, and she came with a friend. Her stature, though small, loomed large for me in the room. I can look back now and appreciate that this was a subtle recognition of her true nature and the extraordinary potential she carried.

A short time later, however, when she began individual therapy with me, she was sitting in my office feeling herself to be very small indeed. As small as a little child and a clearly scared one at that. I vividly remember her asking me for a pad and pen to work with as she fought hard to find her way through the fear. The pad and pen, she said, would help. I watched as she began scribbling...a box? a message? Eventually a sort of house emerged out of the scribble with the word "SAFE" written inside the house. She looked up at me, with the face and voice of a very young child, presenting me the picture as if presenting a sacred part of herself and said, "I need to find a safe place". I understood immediately: She was trying to lay a foundation of safety with me and this room that would make it possible for her to begin the long journey of her healing.

As I sat there watching her draw the picture of the house, the first hints of what might have happened to her began to suggest themselves. Was this perhaps a picture of the house she grew up in, the home she knew before she lost her sense of safety? Was this the house which, at some later point, gave rise to the emotional pain she was coming to see me for? What secrets did this house hold, this picture of Angela's psyche, her history, her dreams, her longings and her needs?

I came to learn that her house did indeed hold secrets. Secrets which until now she did not dare to whisper. Secrets which kept under wraps a story of horrendous abuses. But also secrets which told of Angela's extraordinary courage and the determination to survive those abuses, even if it meant splitting off into many personalities.

It must have been a comfortable house, since Angela's family was considered to be financially well-off. Born in Brooklyn to Sicilian parents, she had one older brother and was loved and coddled as any baby should be. But suddenly, at the age of four, her world turned upside down. The safety and trust she had known until then were abruptly and drastically betrayed. No longer an infant, she began to be initiated into the abusive ways of the family dynamics. In this family, men were to be served while women were expected to sacrifice everything to do the serving. Her father's presence carried with it an enormous sense of threat. The others in the family would cower before him, poised to do his bidding, running around frantically to please him if he should become upset, or waiting with baited breath if they heard his footsteps approaching. Her mother was co-conspirator by her passive compliance. Making her father happy and serving her brother, Angela's mother told her, was to be her job in life. Constantly praising her mother for how well she performed this same job was an additional torture.

All of this proved a potent mix for a little girl who was being terribly manipulated for others' needs, while her own needs for safety were ignored. That Angela had known what it was to feel safe in the first years of her life made the impact of these events that much more powerful. The suddenness of the change one awful day when her father's love turned into something terrible was all the more shattering. This first violation of the boundaries paved the way for ever-more horrendous abuses, and Angela began scrambling in her mind for ways to make sense of things as her world fell apart. Splitting off into multiple personalities was the most effective solution she could find, beginning a lifetime's path of denying the pain, both physical and emotional, to which she was continually exposed.

For Angela to confess in our first session her need to feel safe must have required enormous courage. In doing so, she was daring to consider that her old safety mechanisms—hiding out in many personalities, preserving the family secrets, assuming the blame for all that happened to her—no longer sufficed. For the first time in her life she would risk trusting another instead of trusting her defenses. This was the necessary pre-requisite for her to discover true safety, not merely the escape from danger, real companionship, not only the company of her "family within", and a fulfillment beyond the survival she had long ago become so practiced at.

A Safe Place

The drawing of the house was the first time I would experience Angela's unusual ability to express what she needed for the next step in her healing. This expression was not necessarily obvious, but the symbols, metaphors and associations were always right there to be interpreted for clear direction. If ever there were a doubt about what to do next, her intuition would guide us by quickly pointing out that we were either on or off track. Often, a particular personality would come forth to cue us in about what the next step should be, or at least drop hints as we understood what purpose this personality served, and therefore what need was surfacing to be met, what pain to be healed, what fear to be released.

Once we knew what need was calling out for healing, our task was to confront the fear that had created the need. A locked door, a black box and even a tornado were some of the images that would emerge over the course of our work together--potent symbols of her fear. The door would have to be opened, the box entered and the tornado "touched" if she were to find her freedom. As our therapy progressed, she came to trust that facing her fear bit-by-bit would extinguish it, revealing a new understanding of safety she had never before experienced.

And this, quite simply, was the key to her healing. The process can be expressed in its most basic form as "find and face your fears". Inevitably, they will transform, become workable, even disappear. This is the universal path we are all on, whether recognized or not, whether consciously undertaken or spontaneously thrust upon us as life "happens". This path has an infinite variety of faces. Each of us must engage the specific challenges of our unique fears, as we integrate the fractured parts of our own personality. But there is no escaping the need to face that from which we have in some way "split off", that we may become unafraid of the truth of who we are and what life presents.

For Angela to successfully face her fear, we had to understand the defenses she had erected to protect herself from it. MPD is a defense strategy whereby one escapes the threat by escaping the reality, becoming a different person. To deal with her abuse, she would allow one personality to take over for another when the pain became too great, or project herself into a picture of a different world and live inside of it until the danger passed. Each personality, and there were many, provided a different solution to the same problem: they enabled her to avoid or at least tolerate the physical and emotional pain of her abuse.

The trouble with defenses is that, while they protect us from the immediate threat, they exact too heavy a cost. Taking on a life of their own, they require us to forever lock our attention on the fear, so that we may be prepared to use the defense as necessary. Never feeling secure enough, we build defense upon defense. Ultimately, our freedom is sacrificed for the cause and our true self buried under the many layers of protection that were supposed to preserve our freedom. Angela would become lost inside the world of her "family within".

For healing to take place, she had to unravel the defenses she had spun in the attempt to make herself "safe". Of course, this would only be possible with a feeling of true safety, which we were cultivating in our therapeutic relationship. Understanding the principle of facing fear, she could then dare to resist using her defenses and begin to confront the truths they were hiding. Time and time again, she would bravely enter into the very experiences from which she had previously split off, no longer calling forth a different personality to spare her from the pain. Each time she did so, she discovered the source of her fear did not exist, and she was set free.

Psychologically, this is the task for us all, as we work to heal our past and discover our wholeness. Spiritually, this is the key to recognizing our oneness with each other and revealing the higher purpose of our lives. For without fear, we no longer need to split off from each other, just as we no longer need to split off from certain parts of ourselves. We become "one" with not just ourselves but our environment, finding to our surprise we live after all in a friendly universe. Only our fears born from the past would have us believe otherwise.

Angela's account of her therapeutic journey offers the rarest of insights into the nature of defense systems and how to re-negotiate them for better resolution. For with MPD, each personality literally becomes a unique defense system of its own. That is, a particular personality comes into being for the purpose of defending against some specific event, situation or set of circumstances. It is exquisitely adapted to handle what the other personalities cannot. [2]

---

[2] There is fascinating research showing that different personalities actually effect different physiological responses in the body. One alter may have diagnosable diabetes, for instance, while the rest do not. It is even reported that eye color may change with a corresponding change in personalities!

One personality may, for instance, be very shy, while another comes forth when a social situation requires assertiveness or aggression. The personality called Angie, whom you will meet, is a good example of this in Angela's story. She was the personality whose function was to "have a good time" when the others needed a break from the hardships they were enduring. Her job was to take things lightly, be happy and have fun, even if it meant being promiscuous and at times irresponsible (though never too far beyond Angela's wishes). This was thoroughly the opposite of the personality that was otherwise Angela. And yet, Angie served an essential function and she performed it very well.

For this reason it was almost easy to plot the course of healing with Angela since the information was often so "up front". That certainly does not mean it was easy for her to work through the fears and defenses that showed up. But as she tells her story, you will see the almost step-by-step sequence for healing that revealed itself, as a new personality arrived on the scene just when a previous one had given up its defenses. This new personality would "report for duty" almost on schedule, to handle the next level of defenses that emerged as she dismantled those of a previous personality. You will see how very "dis-integrated" Angela was at the beginning, how many personalities were involved. You will see the careful and elaborate psychic structure she developed for managing her world with the use of these personalities. For instance, you will meet a character named "the Boss", whose function was to keep those personalities called "the little ones" in line, for

Angela believed that these little ones had to be controlled and could not be allowed to express their needs. Every time they had expressed their needs in the past, trouble followed, and so the Boss arrived on the scene to take care of the problem.

You will also see how, as Angela began to feel safe, trusting in a new definition of "love that didn't hurt", she was able to integrate these personalities into a single functioning whole. This was made possible by the fact that she was now strong enough to express and fulfill the needs previously broken up into separate units, put away until some future time when it was safe to bring them out. In so doing, she had to learn how to deal effectively with the variety of circumstances life can bring--as a single, integrated personality.

This integration, however, did not stop with her individual healing. The final part of her journey required her to move out into the larger sphere of life, interacting with the rest of humanity, learning to embrace it in all its beauty and ugliness, despair and hope, fear and love. With this, she discovered the higher purpose of our time on earth; that we may come to peace with all that is and to help others do the same, restoring the original wholeness we once knew.

Let us watch, now, as these ideas come to life with Angela's story in her own words.

Chapter 1

Angela's Story

It is May 27th, 2002, one month short of my sixty-first birthday, and for the first time in my life since the age of four I am *not* living with multiple personalities. My journey to "oneness" started six years ago when I met Dr. Todd Pressman. Early on in our work together, I told Todd I wanted to be a "success story", someone who reached true healing. This was my quest and was what kept me going. And now I can say that this is my success story and it can also be yours. It is not written just for those with multiple personalities. Anyone with a desire to move forward in their life and a willingness to face their fears will find some, if not all, of it helpful. There are three ingredients for success: a trust in a healing power great than yourself, a trust in your therapist and a trust in yourself. I had none of these when I started but through the years, with Todd's help, I have learned to have all three. It was a joint effort between therapist and patient and a process that included learning to trust each other and working as a team.

I would like to take you with me and let you see what I saw and feel what I felt from the first day I decided to "look" to the day I decided to put it down in writing. My pain and cries were kept in a safe place within my mind and body. My memories were tucked away in the dark places that I called "black holes". This is my story of going into the black holes and coming out the other end. A story of finding the light and using it to eliminate the darkness. A process that caused me to doubt myself everyday. Were my memories true? Was I making all of this up? Should I quit now and put an end to my pain?

I had to learn that where there is love, there is no pain. The two were so intertwined that I had problems separating them. Todd had to teach me what real love was. The kind of love that is free to every one of us, the kind of love that has no strings attached. The kind of love that is *in* all of us and placed there by God. I will never feel unloved again. It wasn't easy giving up my old beliefs but it was necessary. I fought each step of the way, letting go a little at a time. A small piece would chip away, leaving the balance of the belief smaller and easier to look at with Todd's help.

There were many times when I believed that the end was not to be. It was too hard and I was too weak. That is when Todd would lend me his strength, talking me through the fear and letting me lean on him. His confidence in me would encourage me to continue for one more day. One more day became my path. One more day was my lifeline to success. One more day became one more week and one more week became…the rest of my life.

I remember the first day I met Todd. I was on my way to his office with a friend to attend one of his classes on *A Course in Miracles*. His office was an hour away from my home and I had no intention of going more than once or twice. My true reason for attending was that my friend wanted to go and was too shy to do so alone. There we were, walking down the hall, looking for Todd's name on the many doors that lined the corridor, when he appeared. A tall, dark-haired young man with a smile that knocked me out. I liked him immediately. I continued to go even after my friend stopped going. I knew by the end of the first night that I was going to start seeing him professionally. Around three weeks later I asked if I could speak to him privately. This began my search for the truth.

My first meeting with Todd as his patient was scary. Talking about one's personal life in relation to the past or present was unheard of in my family. Secrets were common and expected. Speaking badly about family was a mortal sin and could lead to hell or punishment. Whispering about someone, even when we were in the privacy of our homes, was common practice. My mother would say in a hushed voice "The walls have ears". So I whispered right up to the time I saw Todd.

My parents, who were first generation Sicilians, taught me to whisper. Taught me to keep family secrets at a very young age. On the surface I had a wonderful life: A mother, father, older brother, two dogs, bird, a summer home, and toys galore. My home was clean, my mother friendly to others, and my father generous with money. But behind closed doors it was a house of horror. My father was a tyrant and only considered his own feelings and needs. The pain he caused others was overshadowed by his joy when he was the one administering the pain. He was a man who never smiled and eventually taught all of us to do the same unless, like actors in a play, we smiled for our guests who needed to be entertained.

The house of horrors was led by my father but nurtured by my mother. My mother could have been the safe haven to get us through the tough times, but she ended up being the gate-keeper who continually instilled fear in my brother and me to keep us in line. My brother being only a few years older than me learned at an early age to be a survivor at any cost. Sometimes the price he paid was my pain.

By the age of five I started to stutter and had terrible migraine headaches. In a few years I stopped talking altogether. As the secrets multiplied, the stuttering became worse. It came to a point in my childhood where I was so fearful that I would say something wrong, I said nothing at all. No one really cared. My stuttering was so annoying to everyone--they liked the quiet. I did say, "Thank you", "I love you", and "Goodnight". Not much more was required of me.

I orchestrated my first visit with Todd. I knew what I wanted to say and get across. I told Todd how I had few memories of my past. My first memory was when I was 15 and that memory was like a snap shot. My next memory was at 17 when I tried to kill my father. I had no memory of going to school or growing up. I had no memory of being "me". I told Todd I was looking for a safe place. At that time I wasn't aware of how important that statement was and how a safe place would become my quest. I knew there was something different about me and thought I may have a mental illness because of things I had read. I expected Todd to be devastated and shocked at what I was telling him. Instead he remained calm and focused. I must admit that I wanted him to be a "little" shocked. I wanted to know that I had a reason for coming to therapy and that it was not a whim. When I left, I wasn't sure I had made the right decision but I did know I wanted to continue, at least for another visit.

Each week when I returned, I gave Todd another example of my lack of memories. I would tell him about the time I went on vacation with a girlfriend but had no memories of ever going, even after I looked at the pictures. I told him how I didn't remember going to my son's wedding. There were times I would receive phone calls from people who knew me but I didn't know them. It could have been a date with a man or lunch with a woman I met. Todd listened and I talked. I wasn't sure how it was going or if I made the right decision until one night a dream I had put everything into perspective.

Throughout my life I would have recurring dreams where a spiritual Guide would give me life lessons. I loved those dreams. They always made me feel like there was a God. One dream I had was about Todd. I was complaining to my Guide about him and the reply came back, "He is the one that I have chosen to help you. You must stay." I argued with him, as I did in every dream, but I didn't win. He also told me that I would not be seeing him again until I was through with Todd. When I complained, he said that he would be with Todd whenever I was with Todd. So I stayed but at first was not happy. I felt that Todd would never understand me the way he did. I was wrong but didn't find that out until much later.

As I look back now I can see that the dreams were a pattern leading me to Todd. My dreams were a tool used by my Guide to make me ready and willing to face my fears. They were my classrooms and with each dream the message became clearer. In hindsight I can see the pattern but during the actual time of these dreams, I just thought they were interesting. Here are two examples.

My first dream took place in a library. I was standing in front of an index card cabinet that was filled with 3 x 5 envelopes. The envelopes were filled with a powder and on the outside of each envelope was written an emotion. I picked up one envelope that said "sadness", another one saying "fear," and a third saying "happy". I was about to throw them away when a voice said, "What are you doing?" I answered "I am getting rid of all of these emotions; I don't need them anymore". The voice was then attached to the figure of a man. He wore a cloak but the details were vague. I knew he was my Guide. He said, "Don't throw your emotions away; there will come a time when you will need them." It was then that I opened one up and imagined one day putting the powder on my shoulders. He continued, "One day you will be asked to wear one of these emotions and you need to keep them in a safe place until then. You are not able to use them now but I promise you that one day you will wear them with pride." I then placed the envelopes back where I found them and the dream was over.

Another dream had me standing on a cliff's edge and directly across from me, standing on a duplicate cliff, was my Guide. He said, " Jump and I will catch you." I looked down the cliff and it was so deep that I couldn't see the bottom. My stomach leaped into my throat just thinking of the height and I answered, "Only if you give me your hand to hold onto while I jump." He said, "You must have faith in me and first be willing to let go of the ego. There will be a moment when you are holding on to no one, but don't be afraid, I will not let you fall." He then added, "You must learn to trust." I looked at him, looked at the distance that I could fall, and said, "I am not ready." When I woke up I was so angry that I had said no and wondered how I was going to learn to "trust."

A third dream during this time came to be called "Todd's Bike Repair" and is described in the opening of this book. The cover on the book is a painting I made about this dream.

It took a whole year to learn to trust Todd enough that I could say anything to him without fear of punishment. These dreams were my classrooms and not until I was able to move to this next level of trust did the dreams stop and the real work begin.

Todd's commentary

The key to all healing is this: We must courageously find the fear at the root of our problems and embrace it. In embracing it, the fear spontaneously dissolves and the love it was hiding emerges. Angela has expressed this so beautifully when she said: "I had to learn that where there is love, there is no pain". This is always the challenge of growth, requiring a daring spirit that will enter into that which is completely unfamiliar and was thought to be threatening, to discover that we are safe and whole and the fears of our past no longer exist.

For Angela, the idea of pain and love were thoroughly mixed up; her abusers taught her from an early age that their abuse *was* love. They began by violating the sacred oath of all parents--the child's needs come first. Instead, they took advantage of her dependency on them, making her feel that if she were a good child, one deserving of their love, she would sacrifice her needs for theirs. Like all of us, she was vulnerable to such distortion because her dependency upon them was so complete. At that age, she really had no choice but to believe their teaching, no matter how confusing, how wrong or how painful.

This was the beginning of her journey into dis-integration. Again, we all follow this course in some form or other, using fear's strategy to try to secure love. If we feel criticized, we may develop a fear of further disapproval, becoming extra "good" in the attempt to earn love. Or if we have been too ignored, we may compensate with attention-seeking behaviors or clinging. On the other hand, some of us are made to feel too special, too loved. Fear then comes in to warn us that it could all be taken away, as we hold anxious vigil against the possibility of abandonment or rejection.

For Angela, the message was as distorted as "pain equals love". She forced herself to believe that the abuse she suffered was indeed a form of love, desperately afraid of losing the connection with her parents if she did not. This is not uncommon with abuse by parents or spouses, where the need to hold onto the hope that there is even a chance of love can cause us to deny our deepest knowing. Angela convinced herself that it was loving of her to go along with the abuse, to please her abusers in this way. If she did not, she was a "bad girl", not a loving one. She struggled all the way through our therapy with the thought that she was guilty and wrong--always to blame. This, too, is common with abuse, as the abuser convinces the victim that their abuses are harmless, forgivable, or even expressions of something good. As difficult as it may seem to believe, the continuous repetition of these ideas, based on stakes as high as the loss of parental love, can indeed have us believe such things and become convinced of them.

My first job with Angela was to help her see the contradiction between the pain that always attended her experience of abuse and the definition of love. How many times I repeated "Real love never hurts"! Then, as she developed more (appropriate) dependency on me, our therapeutic relationship became the example by which she could start to understand a new kind of love. A love that wasn't accompanied by pain. A love that didn't come with conditions, threats or punishments. A love where caring and giving was an end in itself, even a need. And, as I also pointed out so many times to her, she knew this from her own experience of loving others. For Angela always had a great capacity to love. Slowly, she came to understand that her love was not something to be dismissed because of a guilt she had been taught, believing the guilt would keep her safe from what she feared most--losing her parents. Cautiously, she dared to consider that it was her parents who were wrong and that love may indeed be safe.

When Angela said it was not easy to talk about her personal life, she meant it! We continually struggled with the fear of what would happen--and the guilt over how she was betraying her family--if she were to speak of the past. Once again, only the slow and consistent development of trust could undo this, with my reminders: "Love doesn't hurt, love doesn't threaten".

This "conspiracy of silence" is, in fact, a common feature in abuse situations, and it fed directly into Angela's decision to hide her needs in life. As we shall see, it was one of the primary reasons she first dissociated, when her father threatened her in a dire way if she should scream from pain. The fear of "being heard" forced her to bury all needs, subjugating them to the one need above all others: the promise of love. She would allow all other needs to live only in a subconscious realm where they would later take on distinct personalities that could speak as someone other than Angela.

Her parents' preoccupation with appearances also compelled her to build this defense of self-denial. For her parents used Angela as an extension of themselves when it came to garnering others' approval, seeing her as an object to be manipulated for demonstrating what a wonderful family they had. This dynamic would become so powerful that, when she grew old enough, her father would force Angela to offer sexual favors to his friends to please them, while her mother stood by in tacit approval. Again, Angela went along with all this, believing it was essential for keeping her parents' love. Her stuttering, too, became a useful defense against expressing "the wrong thing", saying something that would displease her parents, finding more reasons to feel guilty.

One more comment needs to be made: As I look back now at our first meeting, it is easy to intuit a higher hand at work: the "chance" coincidence of Angela's attending with her friend, the contradiction between where she thought her life was going and where her deep Self was guiding her. Jung called this kind of occurrence a "synchronicity", sometimes defined as "a meaningful coincidence". Once the therapist (and patient) develops the eyes to recognize such an occurrence, it can become a common event, sometimes offering helpful clues, sometimes merely affirming one is on the right path.

Chapter 2

The Personalities Come Forth

After being in therapy for approximately one year, I was in a car accident. A young man in a pick-up truck ran a stop sign (not intentionally) and slammed into the driver's side of my little Nissan Sentra. Totaled my car, and totaled me emotionally. I went to bed and couldn't get up. I was in a lot of pain and becoming more and more "standoff-ish" with everyone around me. I just didn't want to be bothered. I felt sad and felt like I was becoming little. It is strange to be an adult but feel like a child. I was tired all of the time and wanted to be alone. This developed into a fear of leaving the house. It was amazing to me that, as the fear became more and more intense, my need to see Todd equaled the intensity. Weeks went by when I would not leave my house but to go to medical doctors and Todd. My *need* to see Todd became clear within a few months of my accident when my first *personality* came to the surface and made herself known.

When I decided to put my experiences in writing, I was concerned that I would not remember what happened in therapy during the times that I was speaking as one of my personalities. As I am finding out now, that information is, in fact, there for me to remember. To what extent I don't know, but I will do the best I can to get in touch with my feelings and leave myself open.

Another choice I had to make in writing this was the problem of speaking for the other personalities. I could speak as if they were talking in the first person or I could tell the story by my speaking for them. Since we are now united, it would be easier to speak for them. As I write, the memories come. It is as if they are still with me and giving me the information I need, but they do not need to "come forward" as separate personalities. This is a new experience for me. Todd calls it my " singleness ". I am so used to stepping aside for the other personalities that staying "me" throughout is throwing me for a loop.

I remember the first time one of my personalities decided to speak. Todd and I were talking about my fear of leaving the house, when I had an uncomfortable feeling that something was different. Different in a way that I was unable to sit still. Todd, like always, encouraged me to go with my experience. I then started to drift inside of myself, and felt a rocking motion and a strong reaction that what I was thinking and feeling needed to be said out loud to Todd.

I must admit that I fought the idea because it felt foolish but the emotions and the voices became louder and stronger until my mouth opened and the first *"little one"* spoke. I didn't know it was a *little one* but I did know that it wasn't me. It felt different than anything I could ever remember. The voice seemed to be outside of myself in some way, and I had no control over what she was saying. It was as if I was sitting in on the session with Todd. When she was done, I forgot what she said but still felt her beside me. By the time I arrived at my home, the memory of her was completely gone.

Now I was confused. I wanted Todd to tell me that what I experienced was real and yet knew I would disagree with him if he did say just that. What he did do was to address the concern of the child that had come out. Since Todd spoke only of the issue and not the content, I came to the conclusion that it was just my imagination, and for many years afterwards this verdict was what I lived by. Even when Todd acknowledged my experience of the personalities, I still could not shake off the feeling that I was wrong. Todd was so gentle and so patient. He never pushed me in any direction and let me come to my own conclusion that they were real in my own time. I didn't understand that on this particular night.

I began feeling angry with Todd. The reason behind the anger was not known to me and I didn't care to find out what was going on. I felt the anger brewing inside of me. Each day thinking of Todd without getting furious became harder and harder. I felt a pull from down deep inside of me. As the pull became stronger so did my hatred for Todd. Even though I wasn't sure why I felt that way, it didn't matter; I hated him just the same. I wanted him out of my life and for a long time I tried to run and hide. I lied, but couldn't stand my ground when Todd confronted me. I hid, or thought I did, but Todd always found me. I finally allowed one of the personalities to take over. One that was stronger than me and could tell him to go to hell. That, I believe, was the turning point in our relationship.

Even though other personalities showed themselves to Todd prior to *Angie*, this was different. *Angie* was one of the adults and not one of the children.

There were three primary adults within *"the family:"* *Angel*, *Angie*, and myself. The rest of the personalities were children that functioned inside and only showed themselves to Todd. Some of the *little ones* lived long enough to meet Todd, but most of them died during their short existence.

Of the three primary adults *Angie* was the most outgoing, friendly. She was also a daredevil, and very sexual. *Angie* was all that I wasn't. *Angie* was used to taking over when I couldn't face a situation anymore. She handled men, as well as vacations and all social events. She didn't know what real love was and didn't care. She knew what men wanted and didn't care about that either. All she knew was *she* had to be wanted and liked, at any cost, and she paid dearly. She paid the price with a smile on her face so no one would ever know.

The second adult "in the family" was *Angel*. *Angel* is my guardian angel and from the beginning of my life to the present, and I am sure into the future, she will be there to assist in my spirituality. She was given a body, even though she had no need for one. Angel introduced me to art, poems, writings, songs, and she became the seeker of truth. I would not be able to write this without her.

The third adult is myself. I was created when it became apparent that an adult with the childhood memories would not be able to have a functional life. *Angela* was the person who could live in the present with no memory of the past. And so *the family* was born, three primary adults to manage life on the outside and a multitude of *"little ones"* plus a couple of adults taking care of the inside. The family grew as the needs grew but the three primary adults always remained the same.

Todd's commentary

When one has suffered an abuse or trauma, a later trauma in life can trigger the thoughts and feelings of the earlier one. The Posttraumatic Stress Disorder that Angela developed from her childhood abuse was reignited by the car accident described above. With the car accident, she was no longer able to fend off some of the memories of her childhood. The accident was too powerful a reminder of her earlier pain for it to be kept at bay any longer. This is why the personalities began to "make themselves known" at this time.

As we explored the anxiety evoked by the accident, one memory in particular began to reveal the picture of her earlier experiences: At the time of the accident she saw her face moving toward the steering wheel, as if in slow motion. The feeling she associated with this was of being suffocated. Further exploration led to the memory of a time when her brother would abuse her by burying her face in a pillow and suffocating her almost to the point of passing out. With this, her unconscious began to open up and reveal its secrets. A key had been found to unearth further memories of her childhood that needed to be healed.

Angela's account of the first time one of the personalities spoke is a fascinating moment, if properly understood, describing the transition between "ordinary" waking consciousness and the altered consciousness of moving into one of the personalities. The rocking motion she mentions, I suspect, was the feeling of the "little one" inside actually curled up in a ball and rocking. The "strong reaction" that she must express what she was thinking and feeling is the emergence of the other personality, or the other reality in which this personality lived. We can almost see this other reality pressing forth, knocking at the door of her everyday consciousness.

Angela mentions above that she didn't know whether, in writing this book, the other personalities would come forth to speak for themselves, or whether she as a fully integrated person would speak for them. She believed at this early point in the writing that she would speak for them. At later points, however, you will find that some of the other personalities do speak directly. Even though Angela was indeed fully integrated at the time these passages were written, she discovered that she could, if it proved helpful, still allow this to happen. But it was always a choice to do so, when it served a purpose, rather than something which came upon her as if the personality itself had made the choice. Once the book was completed, the other personalities never spoke again.

Angela needed very little to trigger the dissociative state where another personality could come through. It happened quickly and easily, as if it were something she had been quite practiced at for many years (which, of course, she had been, although never before with premeditated intention). Soon, she was able to drop any "procedures" to evoke an alternate personality. I would simply give her permission to allow whatever experience needed to come forth when such a need became apparent--that is, when

Angela felt herself "drifting to another place" or sensing that someone else "inside" wanted to speak. At this point, Angela would close her eyes for a few seconds and emerge a clearly different personality.

Despite all this, Angela would continually question the validity of her experiences. The self-doubt that so often attends this type of situation, where one questions whether they are making the whole thing up, speaks to the power of our defenses and the difficulty we have in letting them go. For we have built our core identity upon them, believing they will keep us safe from the painful thoughts and feelings we have been avoiding for a lifetime. Angela had been well taught since early in childhood to believe the abuse was something positive, perfectly normal and nothing to be upset about. The voices from her past were like a Sword of Damocles hanging over her head, always threatening. But because her "brainwashing" had been so complete, these voices would convince her time and time again that she must, in fact, be wrong to believe they were anything but loving, and that it was she who was guilty for thinking otherwise.

The reason Angela became angry with me, as she now understands, was because I was "responsible" for having her recognize that her defense systems were not as airtight as she had imagined. The more we questioned the way she had always understood things, and the more the "personalities" had a chance to be heard, learning a new way of dealing with their pain, the more threatened Angela felt as she watched her defenses begin to dismantle. Of course, it was dismantling by her choice, as the internal pressure pushed her to find a better way of handling her past. Still, the habit of being afraid of this past should she let go of her defenses caused great anxiety. Her solution was to temporarily find a new defense—getting angry with me, finding me at fault--so as not to have to face herself.

The three "adults" Angela describes were three different adaptations to living life as an adult in the world. Angie was the personality who dealt with other people and relationships. She took care of the threat that people had always posed to Angela by being a partying, carefree, "fun" person who could get others (especially men) to like her and therefore be safe. Ironically, as is true with all our defenses, this strategy often backfired, putting her in some very risky situations, both sexually and in terms of fulfilling her practical responsibilities. When Angie took over, she often followed her impulses, traveling, meeting and staying with men, and so forth, leaving the obligations of Angela's life behind.

Angela's primary function, on the other hand, was to fulfill these obligations. It is nothing short of extraordinary that she was able to handle the requirements of daily living so well, while at the same time managing the extreme demands of her internal world. She had always maintained employment and proven herself to be a very hard-working and reliable employee. She had even married, raised two children with great success and kept up with all the details of functioning in society. Of course, as she says, she had to erase her awareness of the past to accomplish this, the cost of which was equally extraordinary.

As a side note, it is interesting that she describes herself as having been "created" at this time, since she is the primary personality, the one we would consider the "real" identity, existing since birth. I questioned her about this apparent paradox on a couple of occasions, but she wasn't able to shed any light on the answer. My best understanding is that the adult Angela was "born" at the time when there was a need to function responsibly in the practical world, just as we may say any of us are born as adults after we finish childhood.

Finally, Angel was, as Angela has indicated, a very spiritual personality. She didn't show up often in our work together, but when she did the sense of presence in the room was palpable and very, very special. "Holy" is an appropriate description. Angel's role was to connect Angela with higher realms, bringing the comfort that comes from knowing the pain of the world is temporary and a better experience awaits.

In fact, it is common in people with Multiple Personality Disorder to have such a spiritual personality as one of the family. This personality is one who gives guidance and direction, and can have what look like psychic abilities. At a later point in our work, Angela realized that Angel was what she called her spiritual Guide. This meant that she was not a separate personality that had split off from the whole but rather a more distinct entity that Angela believes was present at her birth. As a Guide, she therefore did not become integrated into the whole

41

in quite the same way as the rest; she kept a certain individuality for Angela to contact whenever she should need spiritual direction.

This "family within" was an essential source of companionship for Angela. It provided relief from her loneliness and her alone-ness. This is also one of the reasons I was let into the family (as you will see, a personality was born named Tang, standing for "Todd and Angela") and I used this to therapeutic advantage as much as possible. For example, on many occasions I would insist that she could not or was not allowed to make decisions without me (when, for instance, she was at risk of harming herself), since I was part of the family now and had to be included in such decisions. This approach was also the beginning of the process of helping Angela know that she as a single person was "real", living in the real world, and having real effects on others outside of her. By having to consider me in her decision-making, she could safely practice giving up the need to separate herself from the rest of the world. It would eventually become necessary for her to let go of her insulated life inside the "family", an illusion within which she tried to have full control over the painful circumstances of the world outside.

Chapter 3

Angie And The Boss

The morning that Todd first met *Angie* was when she called into his office and left a message that Angela was going away on vacation and she would not be back for a long time. In the past, she would tell no one when she made the switch, but it was different with Todd. She knew that he would keep calling until he spoke to someone. So she called him. She had already met Todd on a few different occasions but never let him know that he wasn't speaking to Angela. This time, she thought, he would know because she intended to stay out for months if not years.

Angie liked Todd and enjoyed shocking him. It was like having a playmate. Todd was informed by *Angie* to stop calling the house and Angela would get back to him when she returned from her vacation. He was cool about it but hung on like a jellyfish. *Angie* thought that after a week or two, Todd would give up and life could go back to the way it was. With Todd, things were never the way we planned.

Todd kept calling. He called at work and at home. He called to talk to *Angie* and leave messages for Angela. He talked to *Angie* as a friend who only wanted the best for everyone. This was definitely not something *Angie* was used to. Finally, Todd talked *Angie* into leaving a message for Angela that she should call him when she returned. *Angie* wrote the message on a napkin and left it on the kitchen table. Every time *Angie* would pass the note she would think of Todd. One day as she was going through the kitchen, she read the note again. This time, she couldn't quite ignore it the same way. Only a week had gone by and already *Angie* was feeling the need to "go back". She hadn't had time to party yet and the pull was getting stronger. She picked the note up and put it down. *Angie* did that many times that night until she picked it up and gave it to me. I called Todd to say I was back.

Angie and Todd became friends. And often throughout the therapy, *Angie* would help everyone (including Todd) by stepping in and give whoever needed it a break.

Someone called "*the Boss*" took care of the little ones inside. He was what his name implied. He was "*the Boss*" and had a big job. When Todd met "*the Boss*", he was watching over 70 little ones with an iron hand and acted as if he were tough as nails. He didn't like Todd taking over his territory and felt threatened. He had no problem letting Todd know just how he felt and tried to get Todd to back down and stand behind him instead of in front of him. At first "*the Boss*" saw this as a battle. He felt up to the challenge. But Todd responded by being nice to him and he had difficulty staying angry. Nevertheless, the little ones were in his care and he was afraid to give up control for fear that they would be hurt. All these years, no one had entered his domain and here was Todd whom the little ones adored. It was a struggle, but in the end "*the Boss*" backed down and gave the leadership to Todd.

Todd's commentary

It was a wonderful moment when Angela called me to say she had returned and Angie had "gone back". It was also an important example of the trust that was beginning to develop between us, giving witness to Angela's need to reach out to someone outside the "family" in the hope that real love and friendship were possible. Obviously Angie was trying to restore things to their former state by taking over and kicking me out. But while her anxiety about the changes that were occurring prompted this action, another part of her (of Angela, of the whole) was pressing forth to connect with me. For not only did Angie take my phone calls and engage in conversation with me (she could have simply hung up on me), but she actually gave Angela the message I asked her to. This was the first moment of transformation, of letting me in and giving up her position as the only one who knew how to take care of things when the going got tough. Now she would see me as someone who could assist her in doing that.

Once she became an ally, Angie's help went far beyond "giving others a break". She was one of the primary guides for me in navigating the terrain of Angela's psyche while she was around. Understanding her function--why she needed to be happy, to put away painful feelings and just "have a good time"--was itself important information. But as she began to trust me more, recognizing that we were working toward a new, better solution for dealing with such pain, she underwent a remarkable transformation. Instead of selfishly, defensively, devoting herself to having a good time, she became a mediator and helper when something difficult came up in the therapy, maturing gracefully into one who took on responsibility for the well-being of the whole group.

I remember feeling slightly intimidated by the Boss when we first met. He certainly presented an imposing "figure". I mean this literally, for Angela's physical as well as emotional being would often undergo dramatic changes when a different personality came forth. The Boss reminded me of a classic mob boss and his tone and demeanor were as authoritative and threatening as one would imagine a mob boss to be.

But as Angela said, I befriended him and made him, too, an ally. Once he became convinced that my intention was not to interfere with his goal—keeping the little ones under control—but to help him accomplish it in a more effective way, we became quite a team. My strategy for convincing him was honest and consistent: I kept repeating and demonstrating that if the little ones' needs were met, rather than suppressed, his job of managing them would be much easier. This was particularly hard for the Boss to understand at first, knowing only the "iron fist" method and believing in it firmly. He showed no interest in giving the little ones a chance to be heard, certain that he was protecting them by keeping them in line. He was, after all, created out of a need to take control in the midst of extreme chaos, and to keep the inner family from falling apart.

Slowly but steadily he let me demonstrate that as each little one had a chance to be heard, they could indeed get their needs met. More importantly, he saw this didn't cause them to become out of control; instead, they became more willing to take their appropriate place, having grown quieter and less demanding with the fulfillment of their needs. When this process was complete, the Boss stopped showing up, his function no longer needed.

As an interesting aside, I remember one session where the Boss started fidgeting in his chair and becoming a bit awkward. He spoke in a hushed tone as if preparing to confess something of significance. After several moments of struggle with himself he whispered, "You know, I'm working on getting rid of these". He was pointing to "his" breasts. This was one of the few times Angela's inner and outer reality clashed, believing herself to be a man (as the Boss) in a woman's body. Her resolution was not to accept that there was something faulty in her interpretation of reality, but to try to change reality, as we all do with our defense systems.

Chapter 4

The Little Ones And Patrick

One of the first of the little ones that spoke to Todd called herself *Four*. It was her age and therefore her name. She was the first that "split off" and survived. I remember, when she came out to talk, that I was feeling very small and getting smaller by the minute. I tried to sit up straight to feel taller but that didn't help. At that moment, I kept saying to myself this was all made up and I should stop acting so foolishly. This was a statement I repeated for many years.

Four fell in love with Todd. He was her best friend and her parent. He was everything to her and she felt there was no need of anyone or anything else. *Four* was complete when Todd was there and terrified when he wasn't. Both were extremes. *Four* had only ever known pain, embarrassment, and fear. She felt that she must be a terrible child to have such terrible things happen to her. After all, no one would hurt a four-year-old for no reason. Such ideas began on that awful day when her mother told her that only bad girls cried. These were the words that followed her, and all the others. Todd very slowly and gently taught *Four* that love does not hurt. She believed him, but changed the message to "Todd's love doesn't hurt".

Four had dark curly hair and a sweet smile. Even

though she wished herself dead on many occasions, she was still able to feel warmth with Todd and the other children. She never got older. When Todd met her she was still four years old and thought and acted like a four year old. The memories of her abuse by parents, relatives, and friends were so vivid in her mind that she re-lived them every day. There was nothing else for her. There was no end to the torture. Her pain was so severe that it would make her double over and cry.

But when Todd was there, everything else melted away and she felt love and tenderness. When he left, she would again feel abandoned. Todd would try to teach her to remember that feeling when he wasn't there. The best that she could do was to call him and hear his voice. Even the message on his answering machine would help her to feel his presence.

Patrick was one of the male personalities. He was gay and loved all of the little ones. He was their big brother and someone whom they trusted. *Patrick* was cool. So cool that one of my teddy bears was named after him. He didn't make any waves but gave the little ones a look at the other side of men. The softer side. The safer side. *Patrick* stayed around until he was no longer needed. Anytime someone stopped coming around, they didn't disappear, they just moved further inward to make room for someone else. Picture a personality whose job was now done within the family. His or her substance would become liquid. Their likes and dislikes as well as their memories would become part of a holding entity we would later name Tang.

I remember once when Todd asked *Patrick* how the switching of the personalities took place. Todd wanted to make the point that we were basically one but only thought we were separate. Todd wanted *Patrick* to become aware of his surroundings and see that there was only one body sitting before him. I can't speak for Todd because I don't know exactly what he was thinking, but *Patrick's* answer surprised even myself. He said that all the personalities shared the same space but that was all they shared. They were individuals in every way. When one moved from the space, the next one was able to come out to talk and function.

It brings up a vision of a doorway. Behind the door were my personalities and on this side of the door was the world. Each personality, when needed, would come to the doorway to be seen. A line might form as they waited their turn, but except on rare occasions, there was no pushing and no two personalities would be at the door at the same time.

There was only one time that I remember when this strategy caused a problem. An argument started between two of the personalities. Each one wanted to take possession of the space at the same time. They had to fight without butting in because one had to wait until the other one was done. The fight was between the *"the Boss"* and *Patrick*. Todd let them fight for a while and then joined in the conversation, standing his ground as necessary. He continued the conversation until there was a peaceable conclusion.

Another little one called herself *Six*. Like *Four*, her

name was taken from her age. *Six* was mentally and physically beaten to the point that it looked like her wounds would never heal. She lived in darkness because she felt safer there than in the light. *Six* also liked Todd but was in so much pain that it was difficult to speak. She was the little one that started to stutter and get headaches. During the time that she was active, I experienced headaches and nightmares in abundance. When *Six* spoke to Todd she felt calmer and the stuttering did get better but when the memories were brought to the surface the stuttering became worse again.

Six had a hard time with the fear of being suffocated. She had, at different times, been locked in a trunk, a box, and was suffocated with a pillow. Unlike *Four*, *Six* was old enough to understand that these things should not be happening and looked to her mother for help. No love or kindness ever touched her. Not because she refused it, but because it was never offered.

There was one thing that saved her...the magical kiss. This was a feeling she would get when she was alone in her room. It was a kiss on the cheek that warmed her whole body. She knew when it was coming because her left hand would go up to her cheek and start to rub it softly. The warmth went from her head to her toes and surrounded her with a loving feeling. Whenever things were at their darkest, she would receive this magical kiss. Even now, I still experience the magical kiss.

Every day, *Six* walked to school with her mother, but only until they reached the corner of the school.

Then another personality would take over. Going to school was very hard and sad so one personality was born just to handle the experience. She was called *School Girl* by the others. Compared to the others, her job was simple; she was to take all of the abuse that went on in school without complaining.

Because she stuttered and was heavy, *School Girl* was kidded often and never fit in or made any friends. Her schoolwork suffered and her grades were terrible. One day in class, her teacher had her stand up to read. The other kids were already laughing before she began, so her stuttering was even worse than usual. Her teacher couldn't handle the stuttering and instead of being understanding, she became angry. She opened the coat closet door and ordered *School Girl* to go inside. She did as she was told and the teacher closed the door. There she stayed for the remainder of the day. Sitting on the floor of the closet under the coats ended up being a better place than in the classroom. The problem came when she was ordered out of the closet. *School Girl* did not speak again for a couple of years. The other personalities picked up this practice of not speaking, and no one said anything until there was a consensus that it was okay to talk again.

Crystal was different from the rest. She was blond and blue eyed--special in every way. She refused to acknowledge that she was part of the family. *Crystal* believed she had different parents and was only visiting. She detached herself from everyone and expected to go home at any time. She was friendly and never wanted to talk about the bad things. Like the others, *Crystal* liked Todd and wanted to help him with the other little ones. Her information was always about what happened to someone else. The bad things that she witnessed were beyond her reality. She never wanted to own up to the past. *Crystal* was a princess.

Crystal's drawing of reaching for Todd

Todd's commentary

Here we get a remarkable view into the nature of MPD--its character, motivation and purpose--as a way of being in the world. Angela's descriptions of the little ones comprising her "family within" paint a living picture, as we watch the creation of these various children in response to the needs of her many challenges.

Four was indeed a very sweet and loving personality. Being so young, she represented a fairly primitive stage of Angela's development and her response to the abuse was similarly primitive. To a four year old, all emotions are extreme. When one adds the genuine extremeness of the circumstances this four year old was exposed to, we can understand the "all or nothing" nature of her feelings. Her need for parental love and security, like any child's, was a powerful force in our therapeutic process, as was her fear of abandonment. It was a true challenge to tide her through the period between our sessions, and only Angela's strength made this possible, though certainly very difficult and painful at times.

No less powerful was her guilt, also born at this time, fostered and imposed upon her by the threat of her parents' abandonment. She was continually "brainwashed", if you will, into believing that she was to blame if she did not agree that their abuse was loving or at least justified. This extreme distortion in Angela's mind—that abuse is justified, that she was at fault and that the pain she was subjected to was actually love—was again made possible only by the extremeness of her circumstances. She needed, *in an absolute way*, to make her parents right somehow so as not to lose their love.

Angela's insight about the fact that *Four* never grew up is important: All of us get frozen at a certain developmental age when an emotionally significant event occurs and we are unable to resolve or integrate it. We build our defenses in response and refuse to let life move forward. The defenses become our fortress for containing those feelings which are too difficult or overwhelming to integrate. And so, we literally freeze our emotional development at that stage, and act from there whenever we are threatened in a similar way. Emotionally, we may say, we remain at that age until the original situation is successfully worked through.

Of course, we are exposed to many such events in life, and different parts of our personality get frozen or fixated at different ages accordingly. The "age" from which we operate in a particular instance depends upon the way in which a certain situation evokes our defenses, which defenses we believe will work best. In this sense it might be said that we all have multiple personalities, and only the fully integrated human being acts from an authentic sense of freedom and choice in all situations. Otherwise, we truly act as distinct personalities in different situations, all according to the emotional age we are carried to by the defenses used in the moment.

Here, again, is a prescription for growth and healing: We must work through our fixations, release our defenses, and achieve a full integration of all aspects of ourselves. With this, we embrace the truth of who we really are and what reality is without resistance, no longer blinded and made reactive by our defenses, like puppets on a string being manipulated by our fears. Rather, we choose our response to any situation according to what serves our higher purposes. This is the true definition of Freedom.

That Patrick was gay, giving the little ones an insight into "the softer side of men", explains his purpose; because Angela's abusers were all men (her mother, one might say, emotionally abused her through neglect, as we shall see), she created Patrick as a way to comfort herself about the possibility of a different kind of man. When the dismantling of her defenses had reached a point where her fear began to subside, Patrick "moved into the background", no longer needed as a reminder of this kind of safety.

I asked Patrick how the switching of personalities took place both because I was curious and I wanted to try to point out the discrepancy in logic—that more than one person could occupy the same body. But, as Angela has described, such a logical approach was helpless in the face of a defense system so powerful and deeply engrained. Of course. Nevertheless, there were times at which it was helpful, for instance when Angie was so close to integration with Angela that they felt they were sharing the same eye. That is, both were looking out of one eye together, while still maintaining the separation of having another eye. They still needed this much separation from to keep their distinct views.

I came to understand well the process of switching, where one personality was "up front" and talking while the others stayed in the background. Angela often described the great confusion that would occur when she felt many of the personalities rushing forth at the beginning of a session to be heard, almost piling on top of each other, creating enormous turmoil for her. I assured her and all inside they would each get a turn to be heard, that no one would be left out. This seemed to help.

Another interesting note: There was a time, in addition to the fight between Patrick and the Boss described above, where the strategy of taking turns didn't work so well. It was just a brief moment but one I'll never forget. I asked Angela a seemingly innocent question, and the answer that came out was "yes/no". Two personalities, each with a different need, were trying to speak at the same time. With a slight tilt of her head, one spoke from one side of her mouth, then the other quickly followed with the opposite response.

Angela's description of Six and School Girl shows the depth of her integration to this point. With integration comes insight. Angela has beautifully described her insight of how these personalities were born to fulfill their particular function, serving their particular defensive, protective purpose.

Crystal's purpose was to fulfill the need to feel special, giving Angela not only relief from the pain all the other personalities were carrying, but letting her fantasize about being loved, even more than ordinarily so. But this required the denial of everything going on around her, including her participation in the family. While Angela's dissociation took the form of denying what was happening to her core personality, Crystal's strategy was doubly denying—she would not even see herself as having to deal with the problems at all. She could be a helper, but she did not herself need help.

Chapter 5

Healing Crisis

While these things were going on in therapy, I was falling apart. I became more and more tired. I was confused easily, felt sad most of the time and always on the verge of crying. The tears would linger just behind my eyelids. I walked with my head down and my shoulders rounded. The more I allowed the little ones to speak, the harder my life became. At first I would go into Todd's office as myself and switch to one of the little ones. After a while, I switched on my way in to his office. I was losing control. I didn't want anyone in my life. It was too much of an effort to even try to be nice or try to have a conversation. There were so many conversations going on inside me, all I wanted was peace and quiet. I became very frightened. Strange things were starting to happen. I would be too afraid to open my mail. Mail became a weapon for others to use to hurt me and catch me off guard. I could open what seemed like an innocent letter from a friend only to find horrible nasty words inside directed at me. It would be too late to throw away because the letter had already invaded my home and once read, the damage was done. Bills did not fall into this category. There were no surprises in them, they came every month. It was the personal letter or card that caused the fear. I ended up carrying it with me for days or weeks before I felt comfortable enough to open it. It would go into my car, back in the house, back in the car, for days. At some point the fear would leave and I would be able to read the mail. I found myself checking around corners for scary things, opening my front door very slowly, just in case something was going to jump out and grab me.

At times of distress I would sometimes paint. I didn't paint well enough to have it framed for hanging but well enough to get my feeling out and shared with Todd. The "little ones" carried a lot of sickness and sadness which inspired me one time to paint a picture of what I was feeling. I painted a woman carrying a dead baby and other children falling around her in pain and sorrow. It was like a part of my insides were now on paper, and it felt good for the first time to reveal the pain. I didn't cry when I looked at the picture because I was still unable to cry, but today when I look at it again, I cry.

My nightmares were terrible and getting worse all the time. One of my nightmares took place in my bedroom. I rolled over and felt something in my bed. I put my light on and saw that there was a skeleton lying next to me. The skeleton was alive and put his arm around me to hold me down. I fought with him and tried to get out of bed. I remember he had a hat on and therefore knew it was a man. I screamed to wake myself up. I woke up and started to walk out of the bedroom, when suddenly the skeleton grabbed me from behind and started to strangle me. I thought I had woken up but I was still dreaming. I started to shout "Wake up, Wake up" which I did. My heart was beating so hard that I could hear it and was too terrified to turn the light on, just in case I was still dreaming. Only when I started to breathe normally again did I turn the light on to look around. My dreams were vivid and still remain with me now.

I began seeing Todd twice a week and then three times a week. It seemed the little ones became needier and needier and the work became more and more intense. I felt I had nowhere to go. I could never go back. Too much had happened, and going forward was terrifying.

Death

During all of this the memories were slowly coming to surface. Before a memory was released it was physically painful. I would experience pain in my pelvic area that would double me up. It would continue until the memory was brought to the surface, looked at, and released. This was not an easy task. It never got easier, it just continued. The one thought I kept repeating was "This will not kill me, it will only feel like it will". The memory would start small. It may have been a closed door in my mind that needed to be approached. That in itself was scary and Todd would walk with me being "big and strong". Bigger than anything I could imagine and stronger than anyone I had ever known. We, Todd and I, would approach the door slowly and when I was ready, I would open it. The pain would then start and continue while I walked through the door, only to be relieved once the memory was resolved.

On one occasion, the memory started by my looking at a box. I described the box to Todd: it was big and it was lying on a floor in a cold, dark place. It took a while for me to see beyond the box. The door, I then recognized, was the cellar door and the box was on the cellar floor. There was a figure at the top of the stairs and someone standing by the box. With Todd's help I looked closer at the people there. Again, he reminded me that he was bigger and stronger than anyone I had ever known, or will know, in any memory. I then remembered that I was placed in the box but I didn't seem to mind. I was being punished for allowing my brother to get in trouble. I was only six years old and he was nine, yet it was my responsibility to make him happy. I always had to tell my mother how much I loved her and how much I loved my brother. Even when I was being beaten, I had to say the words. If I didn't, I was punished until I submitted to their request. On this occasion, the box was my punishment. It seems strange to me now that in some ways the box was a safe place. At least I knew that I would be free from the punishment until I was let out.

Todd's commentary

It is a difficult but necessary truth that therapy can sometimes precipitate what is called a "healing crisis". Here, long-buried thoughts and feelings come to the surface in the process of being "cleansed". This can make things uncomfortable for a time, to say the least. The therapist's primary responsibility in this event is to continually comfort and remind the patient that they are, in fact, experiencing a healing crisis, that the pain that has been stored inside is being washed out, and that there is a most important outcome to look forward to. It is helpful to remind the patient that they have been carrying around this pain, even if in unconsciousness, all along, and that this is their chance to get it out. Angela's deep understanding of these things gave her the courage to continually face her fears, working them through to resolution. She was well anchored in the picture of her positive outcome—full integration—and held on tightly to the idea of being "a success story".

In telling of her experience in the box, Angela has not revealed the whole story, indicating that she was not yet ready to fully integrate the memory at the time she wrote this. While it is true she felt safe from other punishment while in the box, her memories of the cold, dark cellar with bugs crawling all over her, bugs she couldn't see because of the darkness but only feel and anticipate, left her terrified. Around this time in our therapy, she came in with a picture, a collage really, that she had allowed the little ones to create. It was a picture of a little girl with bugs crawling all over her. She had a great deal of emotion showing me the picture, making a point to let me know how much the ones inside needed to get this out on paper, even though it was so upsetting. She then promptly asked me to keep the picture in a safe place where she wouldn't have to look at it. She did not want it thrown away; it was a necessary part of the healing process. But she was not ready to confront it fully and directly, needing to keep it at a safe distance from full consciousness. Knowing I had it in my possession felt to her like a step in the right direction.

An important part of the work we did around this memory in the cellar included transforming her experience of the box into something safe. We did this by finding various ways for her to exercise control over the situation, first turning the walls of the box into a velvety texture, then putting light in there when she needed it, and finally feeling my presence with her while she was in the box. Because of her unusual powers of visualization—perhaps the result of her practicing dissociation and generating different realities in her mind—this kind of cognitive transformation was an essential and frequently used tool in our therapy. I might suggest a particular visualization and she would adapt it until it "worked" for her, or I might simply ask her to come up with something that would transform the picture in a way that brought healing. Even if requiring a few attempts, the results were always successful.

But it is crucial to understand that visualization, or "positive thinking", alone will not produce healing results, except perhaps when the injury is very mild.

When the feelings run deeply, when the layers of defense and the belief system built around them are powerful enough, we must, as Angela did, confront the fears head on. This is never to be done to the point where one is overwhelmed; taking on our fears bit-by-bit is just as effective, and often essential, as swallowing them whole. But for true healing to occur, they must indeed be fully faced and confronted. With this, we inevitably discover the fears cannot produce the harm they threaten. Only then are we free, and a visualization can help seal our newfound freedom.

I also took the opportunity to use the transference of the little ones—their projection onto me as a strong and protective parental figure—to help them get through these difficult times. It is interesting that Angela remembers me saying I was "bigger and stronger than anyone she had ever known or would know". This is not quite what I said but it makes perfect sense that the little ones interpreted it this way. When they were afraid of what Angela's parents would do to them, I would remind them that I was there to keep them safe and that I was unafraid of her parents. Her parents could not harm me; I was "bigger" than them in the sense that they were only memories and memories could not hurt. We might then develop a visualization where the little ones could borrow my strength and become so big that together we could overwhelm her parents and take control of the situation.

Insight into the origin of a problem—where and how it all began--is also a powerful tool in the healing process, giving a detachment or distance from the emotions evoked by the problem. This detachment comes from understanding that the emotions are simply a reliving of the long ago past and that the present looks very different indeed. But this kind of insight is not always available and is not necessary for healing. Challenging fear is the only essential task in the path of healing, for it is the only way to discover that that which we feared is not the impossible problem we had imagined.

Of course, all of these approaches can work together: Moving through fear brings us in contact with the defenses that try to stop us from doing so. This can lead to insight--the understanding of the original thoughts behind the fear and the realization that they are no longer valid. Our picture (visualization) of the feared situation is then revealed in its true form—the present day reality that we can now deal with effectively. And through it all, a positive transference onto the therapist as one who cares, deeply understands and can be relied on, lends strength to carry one through all of these efforts.

Chapter 6

"All This Is My fault"

My brother was a victim and a victimizer. He practiced what he learned. I would never admit that I didn't love him because to do so would have brought on enormous guilt. So instead I told everyone what a wonderful brother I had. The best brother in the world. When my brother would hurt me I had to be quiet and not cry or tell anyone. I remember one particular day when my brother was at his best. He tormented my pets and myself until I fell to his mercy. Then he was able to move in and try to stop me from breathing, just to the point of death. It was one of his favorite things to do. On this occasion, my father came home and found me crying. Without asking questions, he blamed my brother. What took place after that was a living nightmare. It will remain stuck in my throat forever.

My father sat on a kitchen chair turned backwards to enable him to lean on the back of the chair to support his weight. He was a very heavy person and always sat in this position. My brother stood in front of him, my mother was already crying and stood on the opposite side of the kitchen. I stood next to my father. By positioning us this way, my father made it appear that I was on his side. Us against them. I was not on his side nor would I ever be. My father then pulled his gun out from his holster and laid it on the kitchen table. He told my brother that he was going to beat him for hurting me. My mother cried harder. It is strange that she cried when he was going to be punished for hitting me but yelled at me for crying while being hit. He called my brother over to him and my brother complied. My father's hand went flying through the air and landed on my brother's face. My brother then flew a couple of feet and landed on the floor. The sounds were horrible -- my father slapping my brother, my mother crying, and me yelling "stop". My brother said nothing. My father then yelled "Get up and stand in front of me so I can hit you again". My brother lifted his body off of the floor and walked to where my father was sitting. Within seconds, my father's hand raised up and slapped my brother again. Again he fell to the floor. I thought I was going to die from his pain or from my guilt. I would always pay in the end for letting him get punished. I now would have to be punished. All this was my fault because I cried and made noise. It was so confusing never being right. Didn't they know that I too was punished by my father? They had to know. They had to. While my brother watched me, it made him happy. I was getting my just due, but when I watched him, it was different. By this time my mother was hysterical and once more my brother stood up for another hit. My mother looked at me with hatred in her eyes. By this time I was willing and wanting to be punished. The wait in itself was punishment. I was the blame for his unhappiness. I was told that over and over again, ever since I could remember, and I believed every word. I was to blame.

Todd's commentary

This painful recounting gives insight into a common tactic used in abuse situations; the abuser forces silence and secrecy upon the abused. Angela's description is so powerful that we can really feel the intra-psychic conflict this kind of suppression would create. The victim has to find a solution for managing the emotional energy, since it is not permitted to simply be expressed and released, and the various kinds of pathology we see, like MPD, are the result.

We can also see here how the distortion in Angela's mind grew, so thoroughly reinforced that she actually came to believe she loved her brother and parents, and that any feelings of upset over what they did to her were her fault, a cause for guilt and self-punishment. We can only imagine the extraordinary confusion Angela must have felt as she became caught in a war of unspoken hatreds, divided loyalties and double-binding messages. Her father gave the appearance of taking care of her and yet was the primary abuser in her life. Angela desperately wanted her mother's love, yet her mother would only approve of her if she let herself quietly be abused by her brother. Angela countered with ardent declarations of love for her brother and thereby hoped to win her mother's favor. But her father made that a no-win situation. Even Angela's attempt to beat, punish and blame herself, trying to show the others she would take on all the responsibility for their needs, was to no avail. And on and on the confusion went. How can a young girl possibly make sense out of all this?

Dissociation, denial and repression became her only way to endure, psychologically as well as physically.

Chapter 7

The First Splitting

When I look back now I wonder how I survived thinking all bad things were my fault. I was never thanked for the good times but was punished for the bad times. And the worst part is that I accepted this from my family. How did a little girl come to take full responsibility for the happiness of all the adults in her life? What could I have done so my brother would not be hit? How could I make sure that my mother would never cry? How did even my uncles' happiness depend on me? It happened, yet I am still in disbelief as to the process that took place to get me to where they wanted me. It started as soon as I was able to understand words and continued until they died.

When I was very young, before the nightmare started, I was primed to be the subject of torture and manipulation. Up to the age of four, my parents kept reminding me how much they loved me, and continued to touch me in a soft and trusting way while saying the magic words, "I love you". I had no reason not to trust them. After all, they were my parents. Behind all the loving talk was an undertow of control. So subtle that even now I have to step back to look. I was threatened each day with the prospect of losing their love if I wasn't a "good girl". I wanted to be a "good girl" because I didn't want my parents to leave me and stop loving me with their tender touches. So here I was, already getting confused with the meaning of love and falling into their trap of being controlled. As I look back now, I can feel the anger growing inside of me. Yet at the age of four, there was no anger, just fear.

Love began to hurt. Tender touches became painful. Trust became fear. Food was used as a reward, and I joined the ranks of a victim. My father was the King, my mother was the Housekeeper, my brother was the Prince, and I was the Entertainment. I cringe when I think of my father touching me. My body hurts and my breathing becomes shallow. I want to turn inward and not remember, but I can't do that anymore. I have to let the memories come so I can learn to stand up to them. This, I know, is the only way to let them go.

The first time I felt pain I was so confused that I cried and looked for comfort. It had to be a mistake. My parents loved me and touching is nice; how can this happen? It started on that day slowly. I was sitting on my father's lap. I never liked sitting there because of the smell but thought all dads must smell like that. He whispered in my ear. His mouth touched my face and he said "Daddy loves you. You love Daddy"? I nodded. His tongue touched the inner part of my ear. I didn't like that. I wanted to pull away but he was holding me very close and very tightly. "If you love Daddy you would like Daddy to touch you", he said. "If you don't want Daddy to touch you then you will have to go away and never see Mommy, Daddy, or your brother again. Far, far away where bad girls stay. This is how Daddy loves you." I stopped squirming. His tongue entered and made my ear wet. His hand then touched me between my legs. At first it was bearable but he began rubbing harder and again I wanted to move away. "This is love", he said. "This is how Daddies love their little girls". I looked for my Mommy. She wasn't far away but paid no attention to what was happening in the kitchen. "Open your legs". I did. It wasn't long before the pain started and I began to cry. That was the beginning of the horror that would continue for many years. My crying made him angry and he began to yell at me for not letting him love me, and how selfish I was for not loving him back. I was spoiled, he said, and he would have to fix that right away. I was bad and bad children were punished until they learned how to be good.

I was brought down to the cellar and disrobed. I was told that I had to wait there until the devil came. The devil would punish me for a long, long time, he said. The devil had magic powers to make the pain go on and on. I would never see Mommy and Daddy again. I begged and begged. I cried and was terrified. At this point I was willing to do anything to get their love back. Anything… "Okay", he said. He would give me one more chance. But only one. This time I must not cry, squirm, or yell. This time I must keep saying, "Thank you Daddy and I love you too. Thank you Daddy. Thank you Daddy". I did cry and scream but the sounds were never heard. When the pain became unbearable, I left and *Four* was born.

Afterwards I went for comfort from my Mommy. She would understand and make things better.

Mommy informed me that being a good girl is not only making Daddy happy but I must make the rest of the family happy too. Since I had no memory of the event that had just taken place I was a little confused as to what was expected. I did know that crying and making noise was not good. I was also told that the pain I felt was okay and should make me feel happy not sad. At that time my brother came into my room and wanted to make me cry so the devil would get me. He wasn't much older but understood a lot more than me. He twisted my arm until I cried. My mother told him not to do that but then walked away. He sat on me and continued to torture me. I again left and *Four* came to my rescue. With that, my life was changed forever.

My needs would never be met again until I walked down that corridor to meet with Todd six years ago. Todd, who became my therapist, my parent, my teacher, and my friend.

Four didn't last very long. She did the best she could to protect me and then went deeper inside for safety, but not before she knew that someone else would come forward to take care of me.

Todd's commentary

I cannot help but express my own pain at this moment, as I'm sure I share with you the reader, over this horror, to see a four year old child subjected to this. To feel the powerplay of psychological forces of this magnitude, and in such a young mind, such an innocent spirit. To imagine the confusion and despair and the feeling that her emotional, physical and even spiritual survival were at stake. To understand the desperate need to come up with a solution, a way out of the pain. Splitting off into a separate personality is not so hard to comprehend after all. Nor is the denial and escape from reality that comes with any kind of psychological disorder, the dysfunctional responses we can all make to the difficulties of life. We are truly indebted to Angela for the gift she has made in this extraordinary account of how these kinds of situations can affect a four year old mind and the development of a person throughout life. It is indeed a remarkable gift for the understanding it gives in how the mind works, what makes it choose unhealthy responses, and how to heal from them.

Chapter 8

Growing Up

Between *Four* and *Five* there were many "*little ones*". Each came into being to protect me from an attack and died when they could no longer endure the pain. They would then be replaced by another. *Five* stayed longer and remained inside with *Four.* The ones that died are heroes to me. There were too many to count, but I would estimate they numbered to fifty personalities. On some occasions it took more than one to survive the attacks. On any particular day there could be fifteen or more *little ones* that were "murdered". Their souls were all put in a safe place and remembered by the ones that did live.

I am sitting here trying to remember the good days. There must have been some good times. Even in the worst of situations, things happen to make you smile and to bring joy. I suppose there were good times, but they were always overlaid with fear. Fear that when the good times would end, the pain would start. Fear that what seemed like a good time was probably a trap. All good things must come to an end, and in the end, all things lead to hell.

Our family was considered rich by the neighborhood standards. We had a country place in Long Island that enabled us to get out of the city for the whole summer. Each weekend my father would bring one of our neighbors or one of his friends to enjoy the country. In one way our summer home was a good thing. I was allowed to have a friend. My mother not only let me have a friend but she also allowed me to go out with my friend alone. It almost seemed like a normal life.

But each Thursday became the end of our freedom. Thursday was the preview of things to come. It started in the morning with my mother getting the guestrooms ready, buying the food, and giving my brother and me a list of things to do before Friday night. I probably worked harder than any other time in my life, even as an adult. The grounds had to be manicured, the vegetable garden had to be weeded and the vegetables had to be picked for canning. The clams and crabs had to be caught. My brother and I started on Thursday knowing that we had to clam and crab until our quota was met. We caught clams by finding the mud beds on the bottom of the bay with out feet. We then dug into the mud, again with out feet, until we found something hard. We would use our toes to hold on to what we hoped was a clam and then go under and pick it up with our hands. I was always frightened to do this, knowing I could be picking up anything, and at times my fears were justified. Horseshoe crabs, snakes, and jellyfish were common in the bay. Just thinking about doing that every week brings up the fear and makes me feel small.

When we caught enough clams we moved on to the crabs. My brother and I would go on a small rowboat we had named Tinker. We had nothing but a line and some buckets. We used fish for bait and tied the fish to the end of the line. When a crab would start pulling at the bait, we would slowly bring the line close to the boat, catching the crab with a net and emptying it into the bucket. More often than not, the crabs would get loose and run about the bottom of the boat trying to escape. To pick a crab up we had to come up from behind it, keeping the claws away from us. I could not do this and screamed until my brother got the crab back into the bucket. It was not an enjoyable time, yet I must repeat it did seem more like a normal family experience than any other time.

Thinking back now it was like we were running a free hotel. We were the servants, the cooks, and the entertainment. Even when one of the guests would want to help, my father would not let them. He was the King and we were his subordinates. As long as my mother cooked enough food and my brother and I caught enough crabs and clams, the weekend would go fairly well. There were too many people around for my life to be in danger from unknown hands. But not from my father's hands. One memory in particular still has me want to cry and to kill.

On one particular Thursday, as hard as my brother and I tried to catch the quota, we failed. My father was embarrassed that he did not have enough crabs and clams to give to his guests to take home with them. He accused us of not doing our job and determined we needed punishment. The guests were trying to keep his temper down by saying it was okay, but my father would not hear of it. How dare his family embarrass him before his friends! He would make sure that it would never happen again. I stood before him, frozen to the ground, my brother next to me pleading for our lives. My brother had more to lose than I did. He would be blamed for a job not done well. My father's gun lay beside him. We both looked at it, waiting for what we thought was the inevitable.

One of the guests that was also one of my father's best friends jumped in to our defense. He reminded my father that at times the fish did not run as well as other times and that fishing in the evening would be the best time. Therefore, he would like to go out with us, since it was already evening, and try again. He convinced my father that it would not be a chore but a pleasure to be able to do his own fishing. That evening not only did this man save my life, but also my brother's. He went fishing with my brother while I stayed home to make sure my father was happy. After all, that was my job. While my mother entertained the rest of the company, I stroked my father's ego and his body. I lived another day and often wondered if that was a good thing or a bad thing.

Sunday night everyone would leave and the three of us would use Monday as cleaning day and Tuesday and Wednesday as our days off. We went shopping, swimming, and played with our friends. Normal stuff. Stuff that memories are made of.

We had this summer home for many years, all of them being abusive. I was six when we started to go there and fourteen when we stopped. A secret place far from everyone where all things were possible. Rooms were built above the garage to house the many guests and to enable privacy when privacy was needed. A place where Daddy's guests could bring Daddy's little girl for some playtime. Everyone thought Daddy was so nice to his friends. And Daddy told me his friends were the best and I was lucky to have them want me to be their best friend. Consequently, *Six* was born.

Six lived for some time. Others came in and out to help her but died in the process of trying. I never knew the men my father sent. Never knew where they came from or their names. It didn't matter. They wanted me to perform and I did, or shall I say *Six* did.

By the time I (Six) was born, the abuse was going on for two years but not shared. It was shared within the family and up until this time, it was kept within the family. I was now old enough to bring the same pleasures to others that I had brought to my father. I was now trained to obey and learned how to endure pain without making noise. As I tell this story the pain is already starting to build up in my body. Pain that I am used to and in some ways enjoy. This pain is who I am. This pain makes me real. This pain brings others pleasure and therefore it is a good thing. Fat hands and fingers touching me until they screamed with pleasure. Fat ugly penises forcing their way into my little body and continuing until they screamed with joy and I screamed with pain. The big difference was that they screamed out loud and I screamed inside. When it was over I had to say thank you and that is just what I did. As time went by I also had to ask if they wanted more or if there was something else I could do for them. I was told I was special. Not every little girl would have the opportunity to make so many men feel so good.

I grew fatter and fatter trying to keep them further from me. I was so afraid I might say something wrong that I started to stutter. My body became the enemy and migraine headaches became the norm. Now I was in pain all of the time and this was a good thing. Now I would get used to pain in such a way that it would only be a difference of degree and therefore much more acceptable. It was on one of these weekends when one of the guests thought it would be nice to see me have sex with an animal. Not a real animal for starters but a stuffed one to practice on. I could not tell you what was going on in my mind because this is when others would step in and help. I can tell you that by now I just didn't care. Why not an animal? After all-- animals are kind and lovable and would never hurt anyone.

Todd's commentary

Of course, in the italicized section above, it is "Six" who is speaking. We can actually see her starting to influence Angela's writing before she came out fully in the italicized section—notice the feeling of a small child coming through. Also notice that Angela was still present in the background through this writing, guiding Six in the effort, "to help her feel safe" (Angela's words). Therefore, some of the writing sounds more mature than that of a six year old, but the essence is clearly what Six needed to convey.

Angela's concern that she wouldn't be able to contact the other personalities in writing this book seemed to evolve, as she and I discussed, into a very natural flow. This does not mean that she had not fully integrated the personalities. Like all of us, we can tap into different parts of ourselves at different times when useful. Angela's ability to do this was enhanced, creating the perception of a distinct personality. But, as in her own description, integration doesn't mean the other personalities disappeared. Rather, they came to co-exist within her, functioning as one coherent unit, losing their need to be identified individually. They became, we might say, "aspects" of the one whole person. Again, this is not so different from how any of us operate, except in the degree to which the distinction between our various "selves" is manifest.

We can really get a feeling in the passage where Six speaks of how Angela's dissociation became established, firmly solidified. Starting with the original threat that if she complained about her father's sexual abuse she would be punished by the devil, she learned to hold in her complaints, her pain and her screams—even her natural feeling of aversion to these abuses--to the point that her identity organized itself around this survival task. "Hold it in or die". With that kind of reinforcement, we can understand how the pain "became who she was" and how it "made her real", even how "in some ways she could enjoy" it. Notice the core thought behind the whole thing: "This pain brings others pleasure and therefore it is a good thing". This was the training that created such a distorted perception, one that was necessary for her survival.

Gaining weight is an oft-used device for self-protection in abusive situations. It offers an "acceptable excuse" for keeping others away, since it is not something one can be overtly blamed for. At the same time, it can give a sense of protection in the extra layers or "armor" it provides. And, of course, the food acts as a source of nurturance, a nurturing one has control over, which is so sorely needed. As Angela grew healthier in our therapy, her desire to lose the excess weight she carried became a natural part of her healing process.

The animals were a particularly disturbing aspect of the therapy. Angela has only hinted at the episode here, perhaps because, like in her therapy, she was not yet ready at this point to deal with it in full consciousness. Later, she will build up the courage to tell in more detail what actually happened, and the importance of the healing it created.

Chapter 9

Angie's Birth, Life And Death

By the age of ten I developed into who I was going to be for the rest of my life. I knew what men wanted and was eager to give it to whoever wanted it. After all, I had no value except to please others and I wanted to feel valuable. I grew fatter but didn't care. I wasn't happy and remained unhappy until *Angie* was born. *Angie* took all of the knowledge I now had and made it fun. I was eighteen when *Angie* became a major player in my life. She was the product of all the training and brainwashing that took place from the age of four until seventeen. Those who knew *Angie* loved her. I started by envying her, hating her, and yet ended up loving her as well.

Angie could not have been if *Ten* didn't open the way. *Ten* began to explore men outside of the family. Not necessarily men but boys. Older boys. Boys that were friends of my brother, friends of my friends, or just someone passing by. Each time *Ten* would confront a boy and please him sexually, she thought she did a good thing. It gave her a feeling of being loved and wanted. They didn't have to come after her. She just thought that if any boy so much as smiled at her, it was her obligation to have sex with him. It meant nothing to her, it was just one of those things.

There was a road near our home called "the three mile stretch" that led to a narrow part of the bay that crossed over to Fire Island. This was before there was a Fire Island. At that time, everything was sand dunes and large waves. During storms the waves would get higher than the sand dunes and come over to the bay. It was a sight to watch, the waves breaking on top of the sand dunes, the water rising and washing down the nearby roads. My family and I could take the rowboat or swim across. It was our special place. The only people that went to Fire Island were my mother, brother, our next door neighbor (Mrs. Trouple) and her two sons. No one else would be there and the Trouples were safe. I was different with them because they only knew me as the little girl that lived next door and we got along fine. I was never afraid with them and until now almost forgot how normal those times were. There's an old saying that goes "Never dirty in your own back yard", so our neighbors both in the city and in our summer home were kept from knowing the truth.

Fire Island felt and looked like another world and it was always an adventure going there. It was a slice of heaven for all of us. I think the high sand dunes gave all of us a feeling of protection from what waited on the other side.

At the end of the three mile stretch stood a house filled with people. Young people, young men, young women. I don't remember how many there were, or even if they all lived there. Some may have been visiting. It doesn't matter; I never did get to know their names or ages.

I remember girls hanging out there too. Pretty girls

that didn't need the pretty men. I didn't belong there. Yet, when the place was nearly empty, I would go to experience belonging to something other than my family. I wanted to belong to that family and I thought I knew how. I was so wrong.

I took my bike there one hot summer day. The first time I went alone I was about ten years old. Three miles is a lot to ride when there is no shade. I was on a mission, and by the end of the day I would belong to someone. Perhaps I would never have to come back. I reached the house around noon and walked in. No one locked their doors back then. I walked into one of the bedrooms and laid down next to someone. I didn't know who and it didn't matter. It never occurred to me that he would not want me. Isn't that what girls did? How could he say no? But that is what happened and I was devastated. It had to be because I did something wrong, I was not good enough and I needed to be punished. This is what kept ringing in my ears all the way home. If I couldn't do this, I could have no worth.

As of that day my life changed from being a victim to being a victim/victimizer. I no longer would complain about doing sexual favors. I would simply get better at it until no one could say no. Bring on the men, I thought to myself. I will drop them to their knees in pleasure. My punishment will be self-inflicted and I will have complete control over my emotions.

It wasn't until I was seventeen and *Angie* took over

that my promise was fulfilled.

I did take over where Ten left off. She was good but too young and didn't know how to flirt. I watched and learned and loved every minute of it. I was good at something and would only get better. I lost weight so I would have a larger selection of men. My only pleasure was giving pleasure. I had some disappointments, but I had some great wins. I must say that everyone liked me and some loved me. No one hated me and no one took advantage of me in any way. I knew just what I was doing. I listened and watched how men reacted to me while having sex. I noticed what they enjoyed most and made a mental note for the future. I wasted no time in getting to the point and, once there, getting it over with.

The stronger I became, the longer I stayed out front. Sometimes days, and sometimes months. It was wonderful. I went to all of the parties, had all of the dates, went on all vacations, and did all of the drinking. Whatever was boring I left to the others. My only problem was that I was never fulfilled sexually with any man. They never knew that. I slept with strangers as well as some boyfriends. I was married once and engaged three times. What a wonderful life I had. Most of the time anyway. I had all of the memories and Angela had none.

The down side to all of this came when the sex was over. The need to be hurt and feel pain was so strong that I had to do something about it. My imagination was the answer. I would close my eyes and put myself in a situation that was threatening and painful. I would feel the pain until I was totally satisfied. I did this each and every time. It was a great solution. The pain was more wonderful than any sex could ever be. Just thinking about it gets me excited. Both Angela and I would feel completely satisfied upon completion of this procedure. It was what we did to survive.

My domination ended one day while talking to Todd. We had been preparing for a couple of weeks, knowing that soon it would be time for me to go. Todd wasn't trying to be mean, even though at times I did wonder. Having me experience love through his eyes was different, to say the least, and believing that love doesn't hurt was the beginning of the end. I realized that letting real love in, like Angela was learning to do with Todd, was a better way to be happy than what I was born to do. And so I laid down my sword forever. I gave a good fight but I was no match for the real thing. Once I understood and felt what true love was, everything I believed in slowly disappeared and I was no longer needed.

I remember the day *Angie* died. She was the first adult to give up her position. She let go of all that she held onto, and slowly disappeared into the universe. It was so loving and spiritual. At that time I thought I really lost her, but I now know she will be with me forever. There was no fear in her dying, only peace. She found a "safe place". "Don't be afraid", she told Todd, "I would never leave you". And she didn't.

Angie lived for 42 years and died peacefully while sitting with Todd.

Todd's commentary

Angie's arrival on the scene marks another major point in the shaping of Angela's "personality". With the experience of rejection by a man, her identity as someone whose only value was to please men was intolerably threatened. Her response was to do the one thing she knew to do and to do it all the more vigorously. She would insist that her defenses work and would try ever-harder to please men, assuming the guilt was hers if she did not, that any punishment she received was deserved. At that moment, she made an (almost) irrevocable commitment to solidify her identity as one who pleases men, and found relief from her pain and her fear by believing she could succeed.

I'm not sure that we've ever had such an intimate view, as Angela gives here, of what causes some people to want to hurt themselves. When she would imagine a situation that was threatening and painful, it was often accompanied by the need to cut herself. This, too, is not an uncommon response to abusive situations, and now we can understand more clearly why. The need to feel pain was not just the result of her need for punishment as a substitute for love, but to relieve the extraordinary pressure of her internal conflict. Just satisfying men sexually, hoping to gain her "father's" approval, was not enough. She had to punish herself as well, replicating the pain he imposed upon her, for her own fulfillment to be complete, if only for the moment. The intensity of this need and the relief its satisfaction brought was, for her, more powerful than sex. Where sex in a healthy situation can represent the physical aspect of love, guilt, pain and self-inflicted punishment served this same purpose for Angela.

Angie "died" because the defense system she represented was no longer needed for Angela's integrity. She had garnered enough strength and inner resource to be able to deal with life without needing to run from responsibility as Angie did. As described earlier, Angie actually became progressively more responsible through the therapy, and it was she who recognized at a certain point she was no longer needed. This was when we began to prepare, very consciously, for her to "die".

On the particular day she had chosen, we were sitting outside. There is an outdoor area next to my office which offers enough privacy that in nice weather the patient may choose to have their session there. On this particular day, a bed of daisies was in bloom next to where we were sitting. Angie and I talked for a while about her "life", our journey together, and what it would be like to disappear into the universe. I pointed to the daisies and said that just as the daisies die and are reborn each year in new form, so would she become reborn as part of everything once she gave up her individual identity. She understood this was true in that Angie would live on in Angela and the family, no longer as a separated personality but as one whose life had helped shape and inform the rest. And she understood this was true in that she would literally join with the life force in all things. It was for this reason she said "I will never leave you", and reassured me she would be present in another form after her death.

I've never attended someone's death before, but understand from this experience how beautiful, how holy, it can be when someone lets go gracefully as Angie did. This "letting go of all that she held onto" is the key to healing and peace for all of us. It is the releasing of our defenses, the melting away of the fear that comes with discovering we don't have to hold on to our controls the way we thought we did.

From the start of our therapy, Angela was looking for safety. She found a significant piece of it when Angie let go. This is the great path, our ultimate task psychologically and spiritually. For in letting go of the identity we have defined for ourselves, that which we have clung to so fearfully and with such control all our lives, we are freed from the need to protect it, and freed from the need to be afraid of losing it. Only then can we discover who we truly are underneath these defenses, and make new choices for our lives from this place of freedom.

Chapter 10

Attachment And Dependency: The Therapeutic Transference

During my years of therapy, I kept looking for groups that would support my process and make my life easier. I was also willing and eager to give support to whoever needed it. I joined one group for people who were diagnosed with MPD. The group was great and very friendly. I was so happy that I found other people who felt and thought like me. As time passed, however, I noticed that there was a significant difference between us. I never lied to my therapist. They kept separate journals, one for their therapist and one filled with their true feelings. Another difference was our belief in the possibility of being integrated. I wanted nothing short of that and they never expected it. Some were looking for a buddy to plan the end of their lives with. I was looking for someone to tell me all the reasons to live. The most extreme example was a group that I attended where people fought over who had the worst week. It seemed they had no intention of ever being happy. These groups did not have a therapist and, looking back, I can see where that can be dangerous. I also continued to attend Todd's group meeting for short intervals. But I just wasn't ready to join in or share my feelings without falling apart. I had to grow some first, so we agreed I would stop going.

I tried talking to my friends and using them as my support system. All of this was done on Todd's advice. Actually, he was pushing me to have a life outside of therapy. I resented it and at times resented it <u>often</u> and <u>loudly</u>. I didn't want anyone else to be my support person. It was so hard to think of pouncing in on someone's life and saying, "By the way I have MPD, would you like to be my friend?". Todd was so insistent at this time I had no other choice but to try. Well, to say the least, it was a disaster. I confronted my friends with my past. They listened without interruptions, and nothing was ever said again concerning my therapy. I think I shocked them and they were not equipped to handle it. So they just made believe it never happened.

It may be important here to note that in the process of writing this story I again shared with the same two friends (Jane and Margaret) who read what I wrote as I wrote it and, in return, I received a completely different reaction. Both of them were supportive and genuinely caring. Both of them cried and hugged me. It felt so good to be hugged. Looking back now I can see that on my first attempt I gave spotty information and my own doubts and fears caused doubts and fears in the listener. One of my friends, Irene, who administered craniosacral therapy was always supportive, yet I did not feel comfortable calling her between sessions. My daughter, Donna-Jean, was my rock. She would let me say anything to vent but would never give me advice for fear she would say the wrong thing. All she would say was, "Call Todd and ask him". By saying that, she knew she could *never* be wrong. To this day, she is still my rock. I love her very much and she still gives the same advice. My son Anthony was not someone I could go to for advice concerning my therapy. But when it came time to start putting the book together, his computer skills were very helpful. Unlike Jane and Margaret, Anthony and Donna-Jean have not read my story or heard any of the details. One day we will read it together.

I kept waiting for Todd to hurt me by throwing me away. Leaving me for another patient who was more interesting, growing tired of the difficulties I was always giving him. After all, I "knew" I wasn't a nice person and was sure it would only take "one more time" for Todd to give up on me. Each time was going to be *the* time. It was torture waiting and even harder thinking it might really happen. No matter how much I complained, Todd always listened and never got upset. I just hated him that much more for not getting upset. No one should be that nice. And if he was, what was he doing with me?

Sometimes, Todd would ask me what I wanted most "right now". It was easy, I wanted to be in his back pocket and stay there. Impossible, maybe, but nothing short of that would do. He would try many different approaches to appease me, but nothing would work. I would get so upset when he left me that I would end up hating him, yet all I wanted was to be with him. I knew this was weird, but I just couldn't control my feelings.

The terror I felt when I thought I was alone seemed

to make me behave in strange ways. Once the *little ones* became accustomed to speaking, their thoughts and moods became mine. My body was not my own and this time I was aware of what was going on. I would feel sad, lonely, guilty, and ashamed all at the same time. Maybe that isn't too different than what most people feel at times, but it certainly was different for me. I did nothing because there was nothing I could do. I was almost afraid to move or speak. So I sat rigid for what seemed like hours until it passed. I needed Todd more than ever but was too scared to call him. Too scared of rejection. It took anywhere from three hours to three days for me to feel that I was back in control. Yes, sitting in Todd's back pocket was the only safe place.

Todd's commentary

It is true that I wanted Angela to have a life outside of therapy. I believed and still do that it was not only a good idea for her personal development, but essential for her integration, both within herself and with the outside world. The struggle we experienced over this was a matter both of her resistance to letting anyone in but me, and my timing. I would not have pushed the issue so hard or so soon if it weren't proving necessary. She needed to build a network of support outside of therapy. Every time I went away, had to change or cancel an appointment, or even when she had a strong need between sessions and could not reach me soon enough, she went through great emotional turmoil. Depending on one person to get her needs met during this period was not sufficient and I tried my best to help her draw on the support of others, but to no avail. I certainly didn't expect her to have instant success with this, but did want her to start getting used to the idea that she would have to expand her willingness to relate to people beyond me.

Angela's resistance took two forms: her readiness to feel abandoned by me, as well as her need to feel that I was the only person who could possibly be safe enough to let in. Having known a world where everyone was unsafe, letting me in was a major step. But as she said earlier, she transformed the idea that love is safe into "Todd's love is safe", rather than looking for more people with whom she could have the same experience. This is why it was so important that I help her eventually discover that others could offer real love and friendship as well, to help her integrate into the "world out there" and live her life to the full.

Of course, Angela's training in self-blame was at work when she said "I knew I wasn't a nice person", and if I were so nice "what was he doing with me?". At that point, she needed to believe she was unworthy, deserving only of rejection and so forth. Rehearsing these ideas was another way she punished herself. The anger at me gives us an interesting look into what was behind this defense: She was attempting to control her world, to stay safe from her fear, by "beating her abusers to the punch". If they were going to continually punish and deride her, she would do it first so they wouldn't have to. When I didn't fit with these expectations, her defenses were threatened. Anger became a next line of defense to try to get me to comply.

Chapter 11

The Marriage Years

During these difficult times I lived two lives. One that everyone saw and one that only Todd saw. It was the first life that most everyone knew.

I had married, given birth to two children, was divorced, had acquired my associate's degree, and worked full time. I was only married for seven years and then raised my children on my own. A single parent. I could have stayed married and had an easier life, but I would have had to live with a man that I could not trust to protect my family.

I met my husband on a blind date. This was the ultimate blind date because I wasn't even aware that I was going on a date. All I knew was that I was going with my girlfriend to the country to meet a fellow she met the weekend before. We traveled by bus--we didn't even know how to drive--to a little bus stop in New Jersey. There stood her date next to the man that would become my husband. We were married nine months later and within the year my first child was born. I was happy. I had gotten away from my past and my family and now had a new beginning. I knew it was strange that I could only remember meeting my future husband and then not remember anything else until my son was born. I never remembered being married and would often look at my wedding pictures to make sure I didn't just run away with this man.

My memory for the next two years is not much better. I was happy and therefore *Angie* was out more than anyone else was. I do remember cleaning and cooking (I guess *Angie* didn't like to do that) and I didn't mind taking care of the house and family. All was going well until one day my husband didn't come home from work. We had been married about two years by then, and when he didn't come home I called the police. They suggested that he may have stopped for a drink and I, being so innocent, told them my husband didn't drink. Around one in the morning he came home drunk as a skunk. I was angry and confused. In the two years of our marriage, he had never drank. I came to find out that before our marriage he was a full-blown alcoholic. Angie didn't come around much after that except for the occasional party or wedding. The marriage lasted 5 more years and through another pregnancy. Now I had a son and a daughter. I held on to the marriage until one day when my husband generated so much fear in me that I had to run.

This was the day my stepson crawled into bed with me soon after my husband (his father) left for work and while I was still sleeping. When I married my husband he had seven children from a previous marriage. One of them, his 17 year old son, was still living at home with us. On this particular morning, I was awakened by the weight of someone climbing onto my body and between my legs. Before I ever opened my eyes I began to push him away and when I did open my eyes, I began to fight. I didn't want to scream and wake the children and have them witness their half-brother naked on top of their mother. He tried to kiss me and I was afraid that I was about to be raped. I pulled his hair and scratched his body until he finally stopped and began leaving the bedroom. He never said a word. I yelled at him as he left the room that his father would "take care of him" once he got home from work. Was I ever fooled. When I told my husband what happened, his answer was "Boys will be boys, no big deal". I now knew that I had to run.

We had a little girl. What would happen to her? Would my stepson try it on her next? Thinking back, I remembered all the times that his friends would come over during the day and try to get close to me. I also thought that he had friends that were not trustworthy. Now I knew that they knew it would be okay by my husband. His wife was up for grabs. I put the plan in motion and got out as soon as I could. No one was going to hurt my children or cause them any embarrassment. I would kill him first. It wasn't until years later that I found out he believed in immediate family members being sexual with each other. I must have sensed something terribly wrong and knew I had to get out of the house. When I filed for a divorce, he came after me with a rifle. When that didn't go his way, he left the state and we did not see him again for over ten years.

When he did return he was sick and dying. He was looking for a place to stay until he died. The children and I gave it to him and somewhere in the remaining time of his life, we forgave him. I don't know how we were able to forgive him but I do know that it was a gift from God, and when God is present, all things are possible, even miracles.

Todd's commentary

It is strange but not at all uncommon for the circumstances of past abuse to show up "spontaneously" in various forms in a person's life. Many times, we seem to have an unconscious need to replay the past in some form in the attempt to find a new resolution. Freud called it the "repetition compulsion". This is why we often pick mates, for instance, that have the same problems as our parents, or jobs that reflect our self-image, and so forth. Angela's marriage to this man certainly mimicked the circumstances of her abuse, with the incest, violence and contradictory messages. But when she discovered he tacitly approved of incest, she realized she was not, in fact, being overly sensitive or imagining things based on her past experience. As she said, she was intuitively picking up real danger signals. In this respect, her history and sensitivity came to her aid. Fortunately, she did escape and avoid a recapitulation of the past. But it is easy to imagine she could have fallen back into the belief that she deserved such treatment, had it not been for the fact that her children's well-being was at stake.

Chapter 12

Mother

About a year before I left my husband, my mother and aunt moved to New Jersey and lived with me and my family due to the increase in crime in their neighborhood. They had to move somewhere and even though I knew it would cause me great unhappiness, I just couldn't say no. My brother had also invited my mother and aunt to move in with him, but they decided that they liked where I lived better. I wish that they would have chosen to living with my brother but could not withdraw my offer once they accepted. I was a grown woman now with a husband and two children and felt confident that I could handle whatever she dished out.

Once my father was out of the picture (which will be described later), my mother ruled the family. I know she intended to continue her reign once she moved in with my family. Oh but this time, I convinced myself, it would be different. I was so much stronger now and six years had passed being on my own, enabling me to stand up on my own two feet. Her technique of using guilt would not work anymore. So the day came and my mother and aunt invaded my home and my life. As I write, tears are running down my cheeks. The beginning of hell started on this day and even after all these years of therapy, it still gets to me emotionally. Old habits are hard to break.

My mother used fear and guilt to rule her kingdom

within the family but showed a different persona outside of the family. As a child I witnessed this and as an adult, I hated it. My mother was loved by everyone who knew her. She was controlling, domineering, and very judgmental within the family, but generous to a fault outside of the family. She had many friends and an abundance of energy. I was her pet. As a child, she wanted to show me off in front of people and keep me tied on a leash when no one was around. She would show me off by dressing me up in expensive clothes and have me behave perfectly. She would parade me around the poor neighborhoods and point out my wardrobe to the unfortunate people who passed by. My memory of myself with my mother was that of a little girl trying to figure out what was the truth and what was a "white lie". White lies were important, she told me. They allowed a person to make up a lie and not go to hell. My mother would determine whether a lie would be considered "white" or not, no one else.

Mommy was scary. My words were to be her words. I had to imitate her thoughts to have her be nice to everyone. Sometimes I would want to say something different, but oh no, that would be bad. She would take me by my hand and walk up and down the streets in Brooklyn pointing to the windows of our neighbors in disgust. I hated doing that and never did see anything wrong with their homes, but I could never tell her that. One day in October we went for one of our walks. Mommy held my hand and would stop in front of a house and say " Look Angel, look at her windows". She would continue showing me how dirty the curtains were and how the sidewalk in front of their house was not washed. I would put my head down trying to make myself disappear. "Walk faster", she would yell, "faster. We have a lot of houses to look at before we can go shopping and buy you something nice." We would do that for many blocks until we walked into a neighborhood where she didn't know anyone.

The verbal abuse would continue for the rest of the day. "Isn't Mommy the best Mommy?". "Yes Mommy". "Isn't Mommy the cleanest Mommy?". " Yes Mommy". "Aren't you the luckiest girl in the whole neighborhood?". "Yes Mommy". If I did things just right, maybe next time she will hear their screams and take care of the little ones. That was my dream. Mommy called me Angel but that was not my name. Angel was part of the birth baby and I came later. My name is Patrick (I was mentioned earlier). I knew that Mommy liked boys more than girls so here I was, letting Mommy know how wonderful she was while keeping the little girls safe. I figured that for each day or even each moment I made Mommy happy, someone was not getting hurt. She never hurt me; I worked hard at making her happy. I made her feel special and pretty. She would buy me clothes and I would just have to jump up and down with excitement. Mommy loved when I did that and for one day, no one cried. I wasn't strong enough to stay out longer but I did try.

If the whole world is against you but you have the love of your mother, the whole world doesn't matter. If the whole world is against you and you do not have the love of your mother, the world is against you. All my mother wanted was for her children to love her unconditionally and all I wanted was a little love to ease the pain. Neither one of us got what we wanted.

My mother died after a long and painful battle with cancer. Her dying released *her* from her pain and released *me* just enough to ask myself why I didn't have any memories from my past. I never would have started my healing journey as long as she was alive. She was too powerful and had too much of an influence over me. A few years after her death, however, I became a seeker. First I was looking for spiritual answers, thinking that would be enough. It wasn't. Then I used the information I received spiritually to ask the all-important question "How do I face my fear?"

Todd's commentary

Throughout this passage, we see the double-binding to which Angela was repeatedly exposed, creating a confusion so powerful she had to split off into different personalities. "White lies" were okay, even if used to manipulate. Displaying one persona within the family and a very different one to others was appropriate. These kinds of conflicting messages force a person to reconcile their confusion in whatever way possible. Angela's adaptation was to split off into a variety of personalities; each personality could understand some aspect of the mixed messages and, more importantly, know how to respond successfully.

The personality called Patrick served several functions, one of which was to fulfill her mother's wish for a boy. In this way, Angela could keep "the little girls safe". Patrick's statement, "If I did things just right, maybe next time she will hear their screams and take care of the little ones", is most revealing. Whether speaking of her father or mother, Angela's entire defense system was designed to please her parents and hopefully get their love and caring. In this case, it was a matter of getting her mother not to hurt the little ones but to consider their needs instead of her own. Patrick was effective at simply keeping her from hurting the little ones.

When Angela's mother died, Angela had an important realization: that it was possible to free herself of her mother's influence--at least enough to begin to look for a new way of being. Of course, the death of someone significant in our lives does not automatically resolve our problems with them. Their psychological influence on us doesn't depend on their physical presence or the continuation of the behaviors which held such influence. In the same way, their death doesn't prevent us from working through these issues, for they live on in our psyche until we come to a therapeutic resolution. However, the death of Angela's mother did represent a significant event in their relationship with each other, allowing Angela enough freedom to begin the process of healing, as she has expressed.

Chapter 13

My Anger Starts To Come Out

During therapy, my mother was always part of the problem because there was not one of my personalities that did not have to deal with her. She was a major part of my life and influenced every emotion and memory. I didn't want to hate her or to blame her. All I wanted was to hear her say, " I'm sorry." It seems like such a little thing to ask to make up for such a big hurt, yet that is all I ever wanted. No one from my past ever came forward to even say " I'm sorry for what others did to you." All I received were denials and jokes.

And I was the joke. Before I had any memories back, when my mother and brother would get together they would talk about the past. One of their favorite incidents to talk about, and to them one of the funniest, was when my father would come into my bedroom in the evening to tickle me. Not just to tickle me but to prove that being ticklish was a case of mind over matter. This story was told to me between fits of laughter. "Wasn't it funny", my brother would say, "when dad would tickle you until you cried with pain?". "I could hear you from my room," he would say, "and wondered how long it would take for you to stop being ticklish." "It took a long time," he would say, "but I bet you're not ticklish anymore." "No, I am not," I answered.

I always wondered why I was put through that ordeal. Only now do I know why because only now has the memory been shared with me from the one inside that held it. The answer is it was done solely for the enjoyment. It was funny to everyone but me. It was meant as the entertainment of the evening and after all, I was the featured attraction. I was older when it took place--around twelve--and therefore my place in the family had already been set. It gets me angry knowing that I was unable to complain and that I was their pawn. It gets me so angry that if I could go back in time and destroy them, I would. They tortured my animals the same way they tortured me and found both to be very funny. I remember afterwards how my dogs would climb into my bed and lick my tears and whimper, feeling my pain. When they were the targets, I would hold them until they stopped crying. We had each other and that was better than nothing.

Entertainment is what I was. Just thinking that now causes a great deal of discomfort. My chest hurts, my throat is closing and causing me to gag, and my head hurts. I don't know if I will ever be able to put any of that in perspective or into a place where I can look at it and not get upset. Entertainment... like a sideshow, or even better, a peepshow. "Come one, come all and let the child entertain you. She may be fat and ugly, but oh can she perform." When this came out during therapy, I was beside myself. I cried. No, I sobbed. I remember looking up at Todd to see his reaction. I kept looking for him to turn away with disbelief. But instead, he never took his eyes off of me and I could see a face full of sadness. He believed what I had said. It would have been a lot easier if he hadn't. Todd then leaned in closer and said in a whisper, " How

111

terrible for you," and meant it. I could see it in his eyes and hear it in his voice that he was sorry for my pain, and somehow that was enough to get me through. Knowing that he could feel my pain was comforting because it enabled me to share this experience and feel his strength with little effort. And at that time gathering strength with little effort was what I needed. "Entertainment". The word still shakes me up and typing it somehow gives it life. It brings it to the surface once more, but this time it is looked at as an adult and not a child.

Todd's commentary

It is clear that Angela's abusers, her father, mother, brother and their invited "guests", were getting a perverse satisfaction from having control over her, or by extension, her pets. This is the essence of sadism. Angela developed a corresponding masochism in order to "justify" their cruel behaviors. She was forced, out of her need for her family's love, to accept this role and adopt a position of submissiveness. Of course, this was attended with great anxiety.

When she looks back now in this writing and feels her anger, she is actually recognizing her power and control, her right to stand up to the abuse. Anger, used therapeutically, can be a step in the direction of healing anxiety; one cannot be both anxious and angry at the same time. Anxiety connotes powerlessness and vulnerability. Anger comes from a sense of power that is resolved to take action against the threat. Angela's anger is an important signifier of her healing, though not complete in itself. As we shall see, letting go, sometimes called forgiveness, to the point where the issue no longer has charge and influence in a person's life, is the ultimate destination. We will see how this unfolded later in the story.

Interestingly, the "tickling episodes" suggest that Angela's family intuitively understood her ability to dissociate. For in tickling her, her father wanted to force her to use "mind over matter" to the point where she would literally not feel the sensation. Her brother, too, understood her ability in that he fully expected she would have mastered this. Unfortunately, they abused this situation as well for their sadistic pleasure, feeling powerful through domination and control.

Angela's feeling of being a pawn for others' entertainment was at the root of her identity struggle. At least from the age of four on, she was treated as an object to be used for others' purposes. There was no mirroring, there was no genuine caring, only the psychological chaos that came from being manipulated. Her solution to the problem was to split off from her true identity as a way to manage her needs, needs which otherwise caused her pain. With this splitting off, she taught herself to believe that pain was love, being used made her valuable, and dissociating was an effective way to deal with life's difficulties.

It brought up tremendous anger as Angela slowly realized that she was not to feel guilty or responsible for all that had happened, but that others had done her great harm. When she realized this, she also realized that her habit of guilt and self-punishment was a way of staying close to her parents and brother, to hold fast to the idea that they loved her and that their actions were justified. This was why she convinced herself she must have been deserving of the pain they inflicted upon her.

Her anger was a powerful antidote to this lifelong defense, and explains why she wanted so earnestly to hear, to demand, that others say they were sorry. At one point in our therapy, I had occasion to say I was sorry to Angela. I don't remember the context but I had misunderstood or misinterpreted something that was important to her. When she brought the error to my attention, I spontaneously apologized. I could immediately see the huge impact this simple gesture made on her, and she expressed how meaningful it was, believing that it was the first time someone had ever done that for her. All of this was part of her coming to learn that love doesn't hurt and relationships are not about being used for others' purposes.

Little by little, anger came to replace her guilt as she realized she was not to blame for what had happened to her. This anger became an important therapeutic tool at various points in our work. For anger that is not reactive but rather a clear perception of right and wrong is always a helpful force, full of purposeful life energy and direction. It can be a potent source of motivation and productivity. It is always safe when used in this way and only a problem when driven by unrecognized fear. In this sense, such anger is actually more about power and freedom of choice, the freedom to stand up for the truth. In therapy, where the task is to move through the fears that have stopped us in life, this kind of anger/power, again, can be an important remedy for fear in all its many forms. Feeling one's power, however one gets there, makes fear small and manageable, sometimes dissolving it completely, as it helps us discover that we are strong enough to stand up to it.

Angela used her anger in many ways. Perhaps most significantly, she used it to move through her fear of giving up the idea of a loving family. On several occasions, she would beat a pillow furiously, remembering the abuse she was subjected to, borrowing my support to feel herself to be stronger than her victimizers. She even dared once, as we shall see, to "dance on her mother's grave", declaring her independence from her mother's influence in her mind. Another time, she made bold and demanded of her brother that she no longer be responsible for their aunt. And yet another time, she found herself in my office almost stamping her feet with the demand that others hear her truth about what really happened in her past, no longer telling her she was wrong for doing so.

It was during this period that she discovered the need to write her story, perhaps to share it with the world, breaking out of the secrecy imposed by her family. She had developed enough courage and conviction in her new understanding of things to overcome the fear that she had made up the whole story or that she was to blame for all that had happened. With her anger she was able to free herself from the tightly held belief that she must be a terrible person for thinking such things and accusing others unjustly. Finally, with a quiet resolve, she came to a point where she recognized that in writing her story and being willing to share it with others, she was free to declare her truth, no longer bound to the "truth" imposed upon her by her abusers. She would be letting go the past and using the energy she had put into dissociation for reclaiming her identity and making her own choices in life.

Chapter 14

Building Strength And Courage

One by one the children came to be healed by Todd. He was now their new parent and friend. He brought them out of the darkness into the light. The journey was not easy.

Four years ago Todd was going to be away for three weeks because he was getting married. Three weeks: an impossible amount of time to be left alone. What parent would go away for three weeks and leave his children with no one? How could he do this? After all, the children needed someone to be there when they became frightened. I was in no shape to be the parent; I had difficulty handling myself without the added concern of a house full of children. The little ones responded the way little ones do – selfishly. All they knew was that he was going away and they would be left alone. I remember thinking that I would not make it and I would surely die waiting for him to return. We weren't jealous of him getting married, we just wanted him to stay close by.

The first week was the worst. Everyone looked like Todd and each time the phone rang we would become hopeful it was him calling to say hi. Maybe he came home early because he missed us and knew he should not have left. If we were good he would not have gone; we must have behaved awfully for him to leave us just to get married. Our bodies hurt from the pain of missing him and then the pain would increase by nightfall. We believed this was a punishment we deserved. By the second week, the little ones went deep inside and all I felt was a terrible aloneness. I, too, withdrew inside as much as possible to avoid the pain and the thoughts of how much longer he would be away. Maybe if I died he would miss me and never do that again to anyone else. By the third week I pushed all of my feeling deep inside and couldn't care if he ever returned. I would see him one more time to prove to him that we didn't need him but then he would be out of our lives forever. I felt myself become rigid and at attention when awake. In my sleep, nightmares would fill the time until I awoke and started another day. It never got easier, it just changed.

Todd returned and I was determined to set him free. This was my gift to him. Saying goodbye was not going to be difficult. Oh no, it was going to bring great pleasure. He called before I came in to say hi and that he would see me soon. I was cold to him because I had no feelings left. It would only be a few more days and I would be seeing him for the last time. I had no idea what he was thinking but I knew he didn't care anymore. I convinced myself that he never cared and I would prove it by saying good-bye and Todd saying "okay."

I never said good-bye and he never said "okay." What I did do was remain rigid and cold for a few weeks until Todd was able to soften my resistance and I was able to listen. Looking back now I can see that there was never a chance that we wouldn't continue on with our journey. Facing my fear and rediscovering Todd's love made all of this possible. This is what therapy was all about and this was what Todd and I were committed to--moving through fear and finding love.

All of these experiences were building my strength and giving me the courage to continue on through the difficult times. Once during therapy *our* fear was seen as a tornado blocking the passageway to a memory. The tornado was so strong and powerful that any thought of going through it was overridden with fear. Todd asked me to step a little closer and reminded me that he was with me all the way. I can still remember the sound of the winds and the feel of its enormity. I stepped a little closer and this time I placed my hand inside the tornado. My heart was beating so fast and my fear was working overtime. Yet I did it and even today I wonder how I took that first step. Placing my hand into the wind caused the winds to slow down. That gave me the courage to put my arm into the tornado and finally my body. By this time the tornado was nothing but a breeze. The fear was greater than the actuality and once the fear was faced, the tornado disappeared. I faced my fears many times—many, many times--yet this time was different. All of the other times the fear was about pain and darkness, this time it was a tornado that allowed me to feel and touch my fear as I never had before.

Todd's commentary

Many of the themes of Angela's psyche are present here, as she found herself in the middle of her healing process with the major "disruption" of my getting married. Often, I would speak to the "adult" in Angela to help her understand that our goal was to learn to deal effectively with reality, including my going away sometimes. It was quite a struggle to build her strength to the point where this idea was meaningful and compelling to her. At this time, the "children within her" were at the height of their need for me, just having turned the corner in trusting that I would be a loving parent. The mixture of feelings of love for me, anger at me, self-blame and ultimately a determination to regress to her former defensive stance of not needing me were all brought to a head. This kind of "transference", where one transfers the feelings one has toward others (especially parents) onto the therapist, is a necessary and fundamental part of the therapy, and must be understood and thoroughly worked through. Even though this was an extremely difficult period for Angela, the ultimate result was productive. She was able to move through the disappointment of an imperfect parent and still know that he loved her. This was a real victory in the course of our effort to help her deal with reality as an integrated adult standing on her own.

The vignette about the tornado is a wonderful testimony to the power of Angela's visualizations and her ability to use them for healing. Of course, she developed this ability as part of the process of splitting off, believing and "visualizing" the resulting personalities to be real. In this example, the tornado represented in picture-form the intensity of her fear. By daring to put her hand in the tornado she was daring to let the fear wash over her, bit by bit, and as she did so its intensity (the winds of the tornado) died down to nothing.

Chapter 15

Getting At The Source Of My Anger

In the process of putting my memories down on paper, the feelings I experienced while reliving the memories began to surface. It felt like hatred was now part of my daily life. I was so angry and the idea of pulling off someone's head with my bare hands sounded good. The anger was building up each day and normal occurrences that would only annoy me before were now major disturbances. It required all of my energy to keep them under a lid.

I told Todd on my next visit that my anger was getting out of control and that I wanted to act on it. Even though Todd did see the urgency in what I was going through, he focused on something else on our next visit. I thought that maybe that was my clue to go ahead with my plan. I asked around at work to get the name of a good place where I could buy a gun and learn how to use it. My only hold up was the money. Guns are expensive and I would have to save up to purchase just the right gun. It would have to be small in size but powerful enough to blow off someone's head with one shot. I am not a strong person so the gun could not have too much of a snap when fired.

The anger grew worse and I stopped talking unless I had to and that was usually a big mistake. I had no patience with anyone and saw everyone as my enemy. They were all liars and pretended to like me, but I knew differently. By our next phone conversation, Todd knew that something had to be done and what had to be done was to let my anger out. He promised me that that is just what we would do but made me promise that I would not do anything on my own until we spoke. I could wait: if not today, tomorrow would do.

I was having thoughts not only of killing myself but doing it so there would be great pain. Getting mugged, raped, and then killed would be so satisfying. Standing on a curb waiting for the "right" car to come speeding down the road excited me. Our next appointment was supposed to be a phone session on a Friday evening. Todd convinced me to come in instead, which I did. He met me in the parking lot and I thought "How dare he invade my privacy like this. It is not his time until I enter his office. Well", I thought, "I will have to tell him never to do that again. People will know that I am going to see him and therefore put two and two together. Now they will know that I am the person in his office who makes those horrible noises". I never did get to tell him anything. I sat down and started to drift.

In the past, drifting meant that someone inside wanted to speak. Since I have integrated, the drifting signals that there is somewhere I have to go. Somewhere inside that requires my attention. With Todd's direction, I allowed myself to drift and went to a horrible place that was full of anger and pain. A place that had never been healed or even acknowledged before this evening. This place was a sanctuary for the little ones that died. There were many and each one lived knowing they would die when they could no longer take the pain and fear. They were the back-ups for the other personalities. They never had a name or an existence except for the event for which they came into being. The place looked like a box. No windows or doors. Since those that remained in this box only lived for a very short time, they never materialized and remained purely emotion. And the emotions were violent and strong. As I was becoming more integrated, I was able to see this place inside of me and for the first time, feel real anger.

I described this place to Todd and with his help, was able to see what was needed. What was needed was not more anger, but love and forgiveness. I approached the box and talked to the ones inside. I asked forgiveness for ignoring them for so many years and making believe they did not exist. I told them I loved them and God loved them as well. I thanked them for all of their help and especially for giving up their lives for me. I reminded them that I would never have made it if it weren't for them. I asked a higher Spirit to enter into the box and give them light. The light was on them, in them and through them. They became one with the Light of the Spirit and joined the universal energy. Once that was done, I opened the box so they might go to heaven with this Angel that had come to guide them Home, and become angels themselves. There were thirty-three of them, more than I first thought, and as they left I said my good-byes.

I felt relieved afterwards and was certain that this in itself would take away all of the anger I had been experiencing. I was wrong.

By the following afternoon I was starting to feel the old stuff again. I didn't want to believe it and tried to convince myself that I was just tired. It kept getting bigger and by late afternoon I was so disappointed in myself I just wanted to hide. I kept thinking, "I failed again". "Now what?" the little voice was saying. "Where do we go from here?" Like a miracle, Todd called just to check up on me. He said not to worry and this too would be taken care of. I went to bed and stayed in bed the rest of the weekend. My next appointment with Todd was on Tuesday and I was just hoping nothing would happen by then.

In the next session, it became clear to me what was behind the more recent anger I was feeling. A memory was coming to the surface. A memory that was tucked away for so many years for fear of living through it once more. The memory was about *Six* who was in a situation that lasted longer than she could endure. Her body was put into straps that not only restricted her but caused her pain as well. She was going to be killed like an animal. She had seen small animals murdered by her brother and larger animals killed by hunters. She witnessed their bodies being hung upside down and knew that this was how it was going to be for her, and it terrified her. She was made to watch a rabbit being killed during a feast and knew she was next. Before she died they wanted to have some fun and, again, she was the entertainment. The names and faces were not known. They were men in suits and women in kerchiefs. In the past she endured all of the pain, but each time it became harder and harder and her body was getting weaker and weaker. This time, just when they started to probe her with objects, she felt herself slipping away. This would be the end. What *Six* thought was the end was someone else taking over. So many layers and "parts" were built, all to secure that I live.

Evidently, I didn't die that day. I still have no memory of what happened next. But after telling Todd about this episode, the anger slowly diminished. By letting him know the "secret", the pain of keeping it in was no longer needed because I now understood it, too, would be healed. Like surgery, it was just one more thing that had to be removed for the process to continue.

.

Todd's commentary

I wasn't alarmed when Angela talked about looking for a gun--I knew she would not get one. Rather, it gave her relief to have a fantasy for escaping her pain, for satisfying her anger. In the language of MPD we could say one (or perhaps more than one) personality wanted to get a gun but the others would exercise appropriate inhibition of these impulses if she ever attempted to put the plan into action.

Meanwhile, I was trying to help her understand the cause of her anger--that she was projecting onto others and the world the "injustices" that had been done to her in childhood. I knew this to be the case because all of the reasons she was angry had to do with injustice, injustice which otherwise would not have created such an extreme response in her. She was outraged at even minor experiences of people doing wrong to each other, convinced there was no goodness in the world. Hearing someone speak unkindly to a co-worker, people with poor manners, drivers who were discourteous, would fill her with such anger that she became extremely uncomfortable and found it difficult to get through the day.

My hope was that if she could see how she was playing out the anger she felt toward her abusers from childhood, she would not feel so helpless about dealing with the injustices of the entire world. We could then find appropriate ways to express this anger in therapy, and she would integrate and normalize her feelings. We were making some progress with this approach, but I didn't appreciate the intensity of her anger at this point. Once I did, I realized she needed a more immediate discharge of the tension, and asked her to come in for a session.

By the time I next saw her I had become concerned that she might try to harm herself (not someone else), for she confessed a rather detailed plan for going out late at night and finding a reason to get hit by a car or become involved in some other kind of accident. I had already extracted a promise from her that she would not do anything without speaking to me. I knew that, because of her attachment to me, if she made such a promise she would keep it.

When I met her in the parking lot for our appointment, she did indeed get quite angry with me. This was her anger at the world--her abusers--now projected onto me, her need to find a reason to feel invaded. My meeting her in the parking lot had never been a problem before.

It was a most remarkable session when Angela discovered the place where the little ones with no names had died. As she has said, it was in seeing this place that she was able to feel "real anger" for the first time. This was, in my mind, a moment of great significance. For such anger was only possible once she could put her guilt into proper perspective, no longer stuck on the idea that she was at fault for everything. She was finally able to look instead at the tremendous injury that was done to her (to these dead ones inside). Appropriate anger at the suffering she endured was one of the first experiences of self-love she had been able to achieve.

Even though her experience of forgiving the little ones who "died" was incomplete, let us understand an important point. The anger Angela had been feeling was now revealed to be the anger she felt about the abuse. And as we have said, she had to contact this anger before she could finally say "enough" to the abuse by others and to the abuse of herself (through feeling guilty, etc.). Her anger helped her feel entitled to be released from the pain of the past, to express all that she had held in. Holding in these feelings, she now realized, was hurting her. Her only way out was through letting go, forgiveness of the whole idea of guilt, whether hers or others. All this was done in the interest of her own healing and her own developing self-love; she could not assume an artificial forgiveness that would further bury her pain. Instead, by asking for forgiveness, she successfully released the pain of those inside by transforming her anger into an expression of love and gratitude. The resulting experience was one of great compassion for herself (the ones inside) and the sacrifice she (they) had made to survive. And although it took some time to fully work this out, her compassion eventually extended to others, even her abusers. This is the power and the promise of true healing, as we shall see.

As always, when Angela resolved one layer of trauma, the next would spontaneously come forth to be healed. As she watched the thirty-three "dead ones" go up to heaven, the next memory was ready to be looked at and worked through. Until she experienced the healing and strength this experience offered her, she was not ready to look at the situation involving *Six* and the animals. But each time she dared to look at what was previously deemed intolerable, she built up her courage, giving herself the message that that which she feared could not destroy her. The result was always a successful integration and healing. Eventually, *Six* was integrated with the rest and in this way, recovered her memories and her wholeness.

Chapter 16

Wanting To Kill My Father

Each personality was born from the previous one out of need and survival. Memories were stored in compartments within the mind and then placed one on top of the other. It would be like looking into an attic that was filled to capacity with corpses and trying to find the first one that was laid there. Nothing was thrown away for every piece had value and every piece took an active part in my survival.

How I was able to survive is still a mystery to me. Not because I wanted to hurt myself but because of all that happened to me. The *little ones* never thought of taking their own lives, but during one period, they did think of taking their father's life. Most children go to bed with thoughts of promises; I went to bed with thoughts of murder. It wasn't just a passing thought; it was a plot and each night I would try to think of a better way of carrying out my wish.

My father always carried a gun and the gun would lie beside him on his nightstand right next to his side of the bed. I would count the steps that would lead me into his room. Since he slept closest to the door, it would be easy to grab the gun, shoot him, and run out before my mother could get up and stop me. I could hear him snoring and knew that he was asleep. Tiptoeing into his room, I would reach over for the gun, pick the gun up and point it to his head. But then he would awaken, grabbing the gun from me and shoot me instead of me shooting him. That is how my fantasy would end. Okay, I would assure myself, tomorrow night you will come up with a better way. We had to make sure that the ending changed and he died instead of us. The next night the wish was basically the same but instead of standing close enough for him to grab me, I would stand by the door. But the gun did not go off. There were no bullets. So again we would be caught and we would end up dying. This went on for years. Not a night passed that a plot was not initiated, and not a night passed that the ending ever changed. It wasn't just a child's wish; it was everything to us. The day came when I was seventeen that all our plans came to a head and not one but *all of us* got together to carry out our plan.

I was to graduate that June from high school. In the past year I had made a few friends in the neighborhood that went to my school. I went to an all girls school out of my neighborhood and was thrilled that I had made these friends. My mother would sneak me out with the pretense that we were going shopping and drop me off at the ice cream parlor to meet up with my new friends. There was going to be a party at the ice cream parlor and I was invited. It would have been the first time I was ever invited anywhere. I wanted to go and would not take no for an answer. My father was sitting at the kitchen table and my mother asked him if I could go. She explained, nervously, that it was only a few blocks away and she would drop me off and pick me up. I would stay out only for a couple of hours and be back before dark. Doesn't sound like much of a party with all those restrictions, but I didn't care. One hour would have been okay. Even fifteen minutes would have been fifteen minutes more than I ever had.

He said no.

That is all I really remember him saying. All the years of holding in all the hate came to a surface. I screamed and then I screamed louder. I told him how much I hated him and at that moment I knew I had to kill him. There was no other way – I had to kill right then. We were in the kitchen; it was easy for me to pick up the carving knife. (His gun was right next to him and impossible to grab). I took the knife and threw it at him hoping to put it in his chest and then into his heart. I missed, but he sat there as if I hadn't. I could not stop screaming and I was told that my aunt, who lived with us, slapped my face to shut me up.

I failed and would probably never get another chance. I went to my room and sank into a place where there were no feelings and no hope. My life didn't change much on the surface except that I stopped talking and stayed in my room as much as possible. My father asked nothing from me and even when we were in the same room, we said nothing. My nighttime fantasies were over and there were no more dreams of being free and being happy. After a few weeks my mother brought me to a therapist who told her to get me out as soon as possible. We continued to live there until I graduated from high school and got a job in Manhattan. I stayed there until one day my mother and aunt informed me that when I came home from work that evening I was to go to this address and was handed a piece of paper with an address and instructions on how to get there. I never asked why; I didn't care. That was the day we moved--my mother, my aunt, my dog, and myself.

That evening I went to what turned out be my new home. We were in hiding so the apartment had to be in an obscure area. It was a dump but it was the nicest dump I had ever seen. It was roach infested and we had bed bugs. Every evening I would lie in my aunt's bed and wait for the bed bugs to come out. She would then kill them and I would then move on to my mother's bed. I felt good about myself that I was doing a good thing by helping out with the bugs. This went on every night until we got rid of them. We had one bedroom and lived on the fourth floor with no elevator or air conditioning. We were free and I thought that from now on, my life would be free from fear. Angie took over for most of the free time and I handled the time at work. That was the plan. The little ones would go deep inside and Angel would go with them as their guardian.

The first major change in my life was when my brother joined the army when I was fifteen and this was the second. Now I was without a man in my life for the first time and it felt good. When my brother moved out, my aunt moved in and now the three of us were a family. I still felt trapped but convinced myself that in time, this too would pass. I was free to go out and have friends, yet not if it interfered with my mother's plans. My personalities came in and out so many times I was considered moody and short-tempered. Once I married, Angel came out to stay to help with the children and give my life balance. Angel, Angie, and I became equal partners in my life.

Todd's commentary

The continual plotting of her father's death was another defensive maneuver to get Angela through her horrors; the belief that there was an end made her situation tolerable. The fantasies about failure in her attempt to kill him were, I believe, a way to prevent herself from actually carrying out her plans, her superego (conscience) still overriding the need to escape from her pain. Nevertheless, this need found a way to express itself by forming a new personality, a personality who separated itself from the conscience of the others. Unlike later in life, where she described getting a gun to hurt others, her superego was not as well formed at this age to fully stop her from attempting to kill her father. As a young adult, she had to find a way out of her imprisonment. Interestingly, though her plan failed, it did force the escape she so sorely needed.

Chapter 17

Spiritual Journeys

I believe that Angel was there with me from the beginning and is my spiritual guide. She still remains with me in that position. She is in charge of healing. (There is a message on healing from Angel in the Appendix).

With Angel's help, around twenty years ago, I went through my third major change and became a "seeker" of personal and spiritual growth. I started with self-hypnosis where I learned two major things: meditation and dreamwork. I then moved on to Silva Mind Control which enhanced these abilities and took them to another level. Next, I ventured into the Seth material which I absolutely loved. It taught me that anything was possible and opened me up to the idea that there were different levels of consciousness. I read it, I believed it, and found truth there.

After this came my studies in the Edgar Cayce material. Cayce, sometimes called "The Sleeping Prophet", would go into trance while lying down and give people "readings" about life, health and the nature of the universe. The friends I made from this network are still friends today.

Shortly after this, I found *A Course in Miracles,* a remarkable psychological and spiritual teaching to awaken the memory of God that lives in all of us. I started going to many workshops on the Course, traveling to upstate New York and studying under Ken Wapnick. I knew I had found my path and felt like I had come "Home". The Course, as I have mentioned, also brought me to Todd.

Todd later introduced me to the teachings of Raj, another spiritual guide. His readings extended my knowledge of the spiritual realm and, like the Seth material, helped me to know that all things are possible.

I was fortunate that Todd also had similar experiences and much, much more. This was a major change and now looking back I can see it was all part of the plan to prepare me for therapy.

Another significant spiritual journey came when Todd told me about "Transpersonal Breathwork". He was facilitating a Breathwork weekend and invited me to attend. I didn't know what to expect but as I said, I had become a seeker. The workshop started on a Friday night and continued through to Sunday. It was a group of about twenty men and women. On Friday night, Todd explained the procedure for the Breathwork: we would breathe to music and as the music became louder our breathing would become faster until our breath took on a life of its own and we would find ourselves in an expanded state of consciousness. We would come to a place where we could get in touch with our true feelings and release bottled up fear or pain. We could also find extreme joy that we never knew we had.

On Friday night we were asked to state our

intention as to what we would hope to accomplish over the weekend. I remember wishing to feel closer to God and gave myself permission to accept anything that would happen. Saturday the group went into a larger room where we laid on the floor and Todd began preparing us for our journey. He told us to relax, listen to the music and just start breathing. He also let us know that we might experience very powerful emotions and that the room might be filled with loud sounds as people felt the need to cry or laugh or perhaps roar with power.

The music started and so did our breathing. First it was slow but soon the music and the breathing became faster while Todd continued to encourage and assure us that all was okay.

Then it happened. I felt my body breathing faster and faster as if it had a mind of its own and there would be no way for me to control what was happening. Next, I heard Todd's voice saying, "Everything is okay, don't worry, I am here". At that point I started to scream. Not just hollering but screaming. I didn't know why I was screaming but it felt like it was coming from deep inside of me and I knew something big was happening. I continued to scream until I was empty and then I rested. What happened next was what I hold onto to this day.

The *little ones* came out. Not just one but many of them. They first went through my pocketbook to search for something to play with. They found a pen but no paper. They wanted to draw a picture. One of the *little ones* asked Todd if he had something for them to draw on and he gave them a small piece of paper. The *little ones* laid on the floor and began drawing. When it was done Todd was called over again. This time he was asked to write God on the top, since no one knew how to write. He did, and I still treasure this picture.

God

Picture drawn during Breathwork

Todd's commentary

Transpersonal Breathwork is indeed a powerful instrument. In esoteric terms it has the effect of "charging up" the energy field wherein, it is hypothesized, our emotional fixations are stored. The breathing seems to suffuse these fixations with more energy so that the normally frozen emotional clusters are mobilized and experienced in an immediate and powerful way. With the emotional release that this provides (if the participant allows a full expression and catharsis of the emotions), experiences from the past, from birth and from what are called "Transpersonal realms"--those dimensions that are outside of what is usually considered to be "ordinary" reality--are spontaneously brought forth in a most meaningful and compelling way. Profoundly spiritual and often life-changing experiences can result, as in Angela's case.

In reviewing this section with her, Angela wanted me to elaborate upon my experience of her process during the Breathwork, particularly about how natural it was for the little ones to relate with me as children, to ask for something to "color" with and to let me take care of them like children. It was always uncanny when the little ones came out; the sense of childlike presence in the room was palpable. Once, when Angela attended a Health Expo where I was presenting, she met my wife who was with me. After a "normal" introduction where Angela was Angela, she went over to my wife and in an instant switched to one of "the little ones". Like a young child she whispered in her ear "Is he nice to you?". My wife, also a therapist with a deep understanding of people and the complex layers of personality, immediately intuited what was happening and replied "Yes, he is very safe". The little one--Angela--got a big child's grin on her face and walked away quite satisfied.

In the Breathwork, the emergence of the little ones was most significant in that they felt safe enough to come out and "play". They were being given the chance to be children, not having to defend against some awful experience, just free to have the nurturing experience (from me and from God) that children need. I believe this is what was so meaningful to Angela in this episode.

Chapter 18

Michael

It was now time to look at my relationship with my brother. Todd wanted me to start thinking of my brother and my loyalty to him and his loyalty to me. I never knew that the feelings of love for my brother were false. I truly believed my ideas about how wonderful he was, and would have no one tell me differently. He was my angel. He was my big brother and everyone knows that big brothers are protectors for their little sisters. I knew that he hurt me but also knew that he loved me. And that was all that mattered. In a world where there was no love, I had my brother. Love and pain were intertwined but that was okay. My brother was the proof of that.

We started by writing him a letter asking for help with my therapy. I asked him to help me with my memories. Todd told me that I did not have to mail it, just type it and bring it in to therapy. Here is the letter:

November 6, 2001

Dear Michael,

This is not an easy letter to write but one that has become necessary. This is a call for help.

You and no one else in the family knew that I had no memories of my past. I hid it well and just nodded when the past was remembered. Little things that you, Mom and Aunt Marge said became my memories and enabled me to talk as if I knew what everyone else was talking about. As I became older it started to haunt me and I ended up going to therapy.

It has now been five years that I have been in therapy and only now do I have enough courage to talk about my experiences with someone other than my therapist. During my treatments it was revealed that I have multiple personalities - which explains the loss of memories. For me it was a survival mechanism and it worked well for me most of my life.

The memories that have been shared with me by my other personalities are horrendous and this is where your help is needed. I know that you remember the past and now I need you to share what you remember with me. This request is not done without first giving it a great deal of thought. I also know that it is something you would rather forget. I am well aware how hard this is going to be for you but I am asking you to put your feelings aside this once for me. I need this from you. You are the only one left that I can turn to and you could give me closure to my past.

You can write back with the information, call me at work (love to hear from you), call me at home, or call my therapist who would relay the information to me in a safe environment. You, of course, could decide not to answer this letter at all. That would hurt me deeply but I will survive. It would be easier for me to validate my memories with your help but validation can be done without it.

My therapist's name and number are:
    Todd Pressman Ph.D.

    XXXXXXXXX

    XXXXXXXXX

Please consider helping me; hope this letter is read with an open mind and an open heart.

Love,

Sis

I was willing to mail this letter until Todd reminded me that Michael might just say no to my cry for help.

Since I never really had to make the decision about mailing the letter, I was able to continue to believe that Michael would be the brother I always dreamed of. A year went by before Todd requested another letter.

The second letter was much different. By this time I was starting to get angry with my brother and doubting my loyalty. The memories were knocking me down with each event that I let in and I was having trouble thinking that love and pain were the same. Problems were coming up with our aunt and

it was causing me to find it harder and harder to stay true to my childhood ideals. I needed my brother to start taking some responsibility for once and think of me. Although it would be hard to ask, I knew what I had to do. I wrote the second letter:
August 13, 2002

Michael,

I have a few things to go over with you and decided that a letter would be best.

First I want to tell you that I went to the funeral home to sign over Aunt Marge's life insurance policy on Saturday. Her policy is only for $1,400.00 and I have put some of Aunt Marge's money aside in the amount of $3,000.00. Grand total so far comes to $4,400.00 and the funeral is over $6,600.00. I enclosed a copy of the breakdown and before I have Aunt Marge sign it, I wanted your opinion. We could cut corners if she is cremated with no viewing. Since you are so far away, I would only have a viewing if you felt that you and your family would be coming to the funeral. If not, I would rather have just a memorial service in the church. Think about it and let me know what your decision is.

Second item I wanted to mention is getting help for Aunt Marge. When Joanne comes down to meet with the social worker, have her find out if there is a program to get her help with going to the doctors, shopping, placing her in assisted living, packing her, and moving her. I will not be able to move her nor am I able to assist her on a regular schedule.

I know you are busy working but so am I. I know you are not feeling well, but neither am I. The only difference between us is that you are there and I am here. It just doesn't seem fair that I should have the entire burden again because I live closest. I would love to see Aunt Marge because I want to and not because I have to. I never had that opportunity with Mom nor do I have it with Aunt Marge. Please reconsider your decision on taking her; Florida has the best programs for retired people and she could get the help she needs.

I will have the papers ready for Joanne when she comes down.

Sincerely,

Sis

Todd thought the letter was good but not complete and I didn't send it. Write another he said--and I did.

The third letter revealed all the anger I was feeling. I had to write it because the nightmares were intense and my daily life was being affected. The anger brewed and I felt like a coffeepot ready to start percolating. I could feel the anger coming out of my pores and it hurt me to breathe. This is the third letter:

August 20, 2002

Michael,

I want to inform you that I have made a decision to walk away from the care of Aunt Marge. As of today, I have relinquished any obligations to the family. I gave up my childhood and most of my adulthood taking care of the family and making sure everyone was happy. I grew up hearing how I was supposed to make sure you were happy and that I better not complain. I followed Mom and Aunt Marge around being the daughter and niece they wished they had. As an adult, they moved down with me instead of you and I have served them well from then until now. Well, in my final years I have decided to make sure that *I* am happy instead.

My day has now come. I am liberated from guilt and so called honor. I have been pushed too far. I asked for help and heard how busy and sick everyone is. For the first time that I can remember, I asked you to give of yourself and you said no. Now I say no.

I promised to get the papers together for Joanne, and I will. That will be the last task that I will perform.

On a final note, I would like to tell you that the last three years before Mom died, I gave up my life as a mother, worker, and friend, to be Aunt Marge and Mom's support. Your occasional visits did not do justice and I swore that I would not allow that to happen again. I, of course, was not allowed to upset you so nothing was ever said. This time, I will do the occasional visits.

It has taken me a long time to come to terms with the past. What you remember as "good old times" I remember as a nightmare. The nightmare is over and I will not submit to slavery again.

All that is left is to say good-bye.

Good-bye.

Sis

I worked very hard not to hold in my anger in this letter out of old guilt. I wanted to mail the letter but Todd said no. Not yet. Another week passed and I was ready for my next letter.

This letter was a two-part letter. The first half was filled with information that Michael needed to know about our aunt and the second half was a declaration of independence. Here is the fourth letter:

August 27, 2002

Dear Michael,

I am writing in place of calling because I have a few things to tell you and I think a letter would be better than a phone call.

First of all I want to tell you that I have transferred Aunt Marge's life insurance over to the funeral home to avoid problems getting her on Medicaid. Since you live in Florida and the rest of your family lives in Long Island, I was thinking of only having a memorial mass for Aunt Marge. Her insurance will not cover a viewing and such. I want to give you the opportunity to give me your opinion on this matter.

Also she will be getting nurses three times a week for the next 8 weeks. If she is not on Medicaid by then, the nurses will stop coming. I was also informed that when the gentleman comes over from Medicaid, Joanne is to tell him that Aunt Marge needs to go on Jersey Care Medicaid and Assisted Living. With Jersey Care Medicaid, she will be able to continue getting someone to come over to help her.

The report from the doctor was good. The only problem with Aunt Marge is that she is not eating and we don't know why. She is down to 117 pounds and her bones are sticking out. The nurse told me that it is common for someone to lose their appetite when the mind starts going. They just forget to eat.

I want to thank you for the help you have provided so far and hope it continues. She will have to be packed and moved. If we only have a memorial mass for Aunt Marge, I will have enough money to hire a professional to do the moving and packing. Aunt Marge told me yesterday that she plans on visiting you soon. Is this true? If it is true, when are you planning on having her visit?

A very important issue came up during our last conversation that needs to be addressed in this letter. It may be hard to swallow at first, but please read it through with an open mind and an open heart.

One of your statements the last time we spoke ran chills down my spine. Calling the past "the good old days" made me shiver. I have been in therapy for over six years trying to get over the past and the nightmarish memories and you called it "the good old days". Due to the past, I developed multiple personalities. During my childhood, around the age of four, I experienced my first personality and through the years they have increased to the total of seventy-two. A drastic measure to solve a drastic childhood. The abuse I suffered emotionally and physically did its damage and now I refuse to make believe it never happened. I am even going one step further by writing it all down and telling people. My story and my healing may help others get the courage to go for help and acknowledge their past. Unless you have completely different memories than me, I don't understand that remark.

You were a victim as well as a victimizer and I forgive both. We were both victims and victims do bond in a special way. I cried for you as well as myself and then healed all memories. Until today, I had a dream that you and I would be the brother and sister that I always dreamt about. A brother that would put me first above all and be my protector. I kept saying, "One day this will happen." Now I know that it was a child's dream. Waiting for the dream to happen caused me to be afraid to talk to you honestly. In my final years on this earth I plan on living in the truth instead of denying the past. I plan on kicking the past in its ass. I would love to have you with me as two adults that shared the same past and therefore understand each other like no one else could. That decision is yours and I will honor any decision you make, as I know you will honor mine.

When Mom was alive I was never allowed to say anything to you that might upset you in any way. I was repeatedly told that keeping you happy and peaceful was the most important job that all of us had. When Mom died I was reminded of this by Aunt Marge. I could have used your help and support during those hard times with Mom but that would have made her upset. Things are different now and I am telling you that my happiness and peace of mind is worth just as much as yours is. I paid my dues and I am done protecting you. You may have never asked to be protected, but it was a way of life for me. Loving you made it easy.

I hope this letter is read with an understanding of the true intent with which it was written.

Love,

Sis

Looking back on this letter, I see how different the tone is from the previous letters. So much of the anger is gone and I felt a quiet strength I never had before this point. I realize I didn't need my anger as much to stand up for myself since my guilt was leaving me. I was starting to understand that I simply deserved these things.

Since the first half of this letter had to be sent and the second may have still needed work, I mailed the first half of the letter only. I had decided to send the second half by itself as soon as Todd approved it. It was never sent.

I wrote Todd the following email out of my need to say what was in that second half.

Todd,

I need to send the letter to my brother now. The reasons will be clear to you once you read the following:

1. My brother needs to know about Aunt Marge as soon as possible so he can make the necessary arrangements and get back to me about the funeral.
2. My brother's reaction cannot be anticipated.
3. My reaction to my brother's reaction cannot be anticipated.
4. Whatever his response is and how I take it will be handled at that time and should not be a factor in sending the letter.
5. I truly believe that I can get over anything with your help.
6. My fears are normal fears and nothing else. Anyone in my situation would be going through the same anxiety.

If you need more reasons, let me know. If I left something out, let me know. I know you told me to sit on it but I can't.

Angela

I still did not send this letter but waited until I saw Todd to decide what to do. But by our next appointment, I was over the need to hurt my brother. We had done a lot of work and forgiving was the essential tone of our sessions. I didn't need to tell my brother what he already knew. I was the one that was in denial concerning our past relationship and I was the one that had to face the truth that my brother was part of the problem. Hurting him now would not help me but it did help to admit to myself that he hurt me and that love with pain was not okay. I would have no emotional ties to him now. He would be someone from my past and if one day he wished to come to me admitting the truth, I would be here. Until then, I would let him go.

The letters telling my brother how angry I was were never sent. More work had to be done before I could confront my brother and stand my ground. Over a year passed before I heard from him again and old wounds immediately came to surface. During the past year and a half, anger took over my love for my brother, but I needed to feel angry and also needed to acknowledge the fact that I indeed had every right to feel anger. So even though I thought my work with him was done, it was not.

It happened when my brother sent me a Christmas card and wrote a few words on the bottom under his name. It said, "Let's be friends". It was like my breath at that moment was taken from me and I became frozen where I stood. How dare he write something so nice to me when I was still in a state of anger! Not this time, I said, will he convince me that he was sorry and I should forgive him.

When I was young I forgave my brother each and every time he hurt me. I would still be crying from the pain yet tell him "It's okay, I forgive you". My brother would then hold me as if he really did love me and that was enough. All the pain was worth that hug because without the pain, there was no hug and that was even worse.

Not this time, I thought. A promise of a hug is not acceptable. I want more. Five days went by feeling confident that this time would be different. I had to decide what I wanted from my relationship with my brother. It was really quite easy to come up with an answer--I wanted him to say that he was sorry that I suffered so as his sister. I mentioned earlier that my brother was both a victim and a victimizer and I understood that even as a child. My brother would wave love in front of me like a flag and promise that if I forgave him just this once, his love would be mine. It was a trick that I fell for every time. I wanted a big brother to love and share my thoughts with. A big brother who would protect me.

And then I started to think of forgiveness and how the word had developed throughout my years of therapy. When I was younger it was used as a way to get love: I would forgive my brother so he would love me for it and be the big brother I had always wanted. Now forgiveness had a much deeper and spiritual meaning. Forgiveness now represented accepting love when offered and feeling confident enough to offer love when accepted. I was not yet in the place where I could accept what he was offering in the Christmas card with a whole heart. But I could see myself daring to acknowledge it. I realized, then, that the big brother I had always wanted did not exist in my childhood nor does he exist now. Undoing the past was impossible. But maybe I could find a way to fit him into the present.

Todd's commentary

When I suggested Angela write the first letter to her brother, it was very clear to me that he would probably feel too threatened to respond the way she wanted. My real intention was to have Angela put into action the idea that she was entitled to speak her truth, no longer obliged to keep the family secrets.

The realization that he might not respond favorably to the letter threw Angela for a loop, putting her in touch with the fear of others' disapproval if she expressed her needs, no longer being silent. And this was the point; to have her confront and become less afraid of this possibility over time. Knowing she was not ready to send such a letter, I convinced her to hold onto it until she was prepared for any response. I told her we would work on building up her sense of entitlement and power (contacting her anger to overcome her guilt if someone had a condemning response), so she could stand firmly in her truth, no longer sacrificing herself for others.

It may not be readily apparent, but the second letter represents a considerable amount of work and growth on Angela's part, as she dared to assert her needs to a much greater extent than ever before. As she said, her anger was building and she was realizing the depth of her exhaustion from having tried for so long to please her brother with no success. She therefore attempted in this letter to cast some of his responsibility for their aunt, which she had been assuming, back onto him, with as much entitlement as she could muster. As you see, she had not yet fully "arrived".

When Angela said I encouraged her to write another letter, my actual instruction was for her to practice, in a letter which she would not necessarily send, a much greater expression of her feelings and the "demands" which would accompany them.

While waiting for me to "approve" the second half of her fourth letter, Angela sent the e-mail to me shown above. The urgency and insistence in the tone of the email speaks to the anger that had reached its peak and her absolute need to express it, rather than hold it in any longer. As with her other episodes of anger, this was a corrective experience. It signified the release of the anger she had been turning against herself with a lifetime of guilt and self-blame.

When I discussed the e-mail with Angela, I helped her understand why she felt such internal pressure to send the letter. I put it in the context of her therapeutic process, rather than the practical reasons she had listed. With this, she understood for the first time what I had been working toward with the letters--the development of her ability to take care of herself, no longer vulnerable to the dictates of her family. And as she understood this, she grew quiet and was able to see deeply into what she had previously been blind to: that her feeling of obligation to her family was the result of their "brainwashing", rather than an absolute truth that must be adhered to at all costs. This was an extremely liberating experience for her, making a resolution to this stage of her work possible.

This story is a living text; the writing of it was very much a part of Angela's therapeutic process. For in doing so, she was daring to tell the world "the family's secrets" and declare her autonomy from them. Therefore, in the course of writing her story—during which time we were still engaged in therapy—much of what she wrote about evolved and deepened from the time she originally wrote it. When Angela believed that she had come to peace with her brother and no longer needed to express her anger to him, she had indeed come to a level of completion with the situation, even though she later unearthed further work that needed to be done.

Chapter 19

Pulling Out Another Memory

Just before the last letter to my brother was the time when my anger had come to a boiling point and I was looking for a gun. I knew that I would explode like a volcano and do something I would be sorry for if I didn't address this issue and do it fast. I spoke to Todd about this very thing and told him I knew how serial killers fell. It feels as if just hurting or killing one person would not be enough. The anger is so great that once you start, you have to continue until it is spent. I had visions of killing maybe ten or twenty people all within the same timeframe and never even thought of the consequences. I felt it overpowering me and growing each day or even worse, every minute. I had a plan. I would go out and buy a gun. I asked around work and they told me a good place to go that was fair and close to home. They also gave lessons on how to take care of your gun as well as shooting lessons. Perfect. Everything was falling into place. I was going to do it and I started to get excited about the prospects of shooting all of those people. I would start saving my money for the gun and start planning on the area I would use to do my killing.

I actually had two plans. One that I would kill until I was satisfied and then be done with it, the other was to kill a little at a time. No one I knew. Just men. Maybe men that no one cared about anyway. Drunks and street people. Men that cheated on their wives, or men that would be willing to go to bed with me. This was going to work. I just knew it. Todd didn't care, I was sure of it. He would understand and let me do what was necessary to relieve my pain. After all, I did tell him about the anger and he didn't say anything about it that made me think he could handle this problem. I decided to tell him my plan just in case I was killed or arrested in carrying it out, so he would understand. I might not tell him all of it. It would depend on how he reacted to what I did tell him.

The following session started off by going over how I was feeling since the week before. It seemed like Todd had an agenda and I listened for awhile until I thought I was going to burst. I then told him that there was something we had to discuss tonight and it couldn't wait another day. I remember Todd leaning forward and saying, "Then let's do it". I wonder what would have happened if I hadn't told Todd and did carry out my plan. Thinking back now, I am sure that I wanted Todd to fix this problem as he always fixed all the others.

I had walked into his office in terrible physical pain. The pain was lodged between my legs and even though it was not the first time I experienced it, this was the worst yet. I couldn't sit and so Todd did what he always does--he took care of the most immediate problem: my body being in pain. Pain that lodged itself between my legs and went from a dull pressure to a pain that doubled me over. Whatever we had been working on had to stop to take care of this pain. Todd suggested we go into this pain and bring it forward so we could heal it. "What does it feel like?", he asked. I thought for a moment while the pain was increasing and I was shifting my weight trying to get comfortable. "It has to come out," I said. " I have to pull it out", I continued. Todd encouraged me to do what was necessary to relieve the pain. I placed my hands between my legs and started to pull the pain out. It was an animal. It was covered with dirt and as I pulled the animal out the pain would calm down for a few moments and then increase again. Another animal and then another one was pulled out, all with the same results. I did this until the pain was gone and I was exhausted.

I felt the animals needed to be cleaned and then set free. The animals represented memories held deep inside of me, memories of when animals were placed between my legs and encouraged to enter. Some did and some did not. It all seemed okay because I loved them and knew they did not know what they were doing. But the pain of each memory was stored inside of me and had manifested here as the animals coming out--as I pulled out each animal, I was pulling out this pain. It was as if the pain had stuck to my insides and was wrapped around the memory. By cleaning the animals, I literally washed away the pain, and as I cleaned them, with Todd's help, I washed my memories as well. I had held the animals safely in my heart and released them on the day I pulled them from within, washed them, and set them free. I was not only free from physical pain but I was free from the emotional pain of a memory I didn't want to remember.

Todd's commentary

Once again, that Angela was contacting her anger was a positive development and absolutely essential for her recovery. It was this anger that would have her translate a lifetime of self-blame into the recognition that she was innocent. We had to externalize this anger so she would stop turning it against herself, causing her to re-experience the pain over and over with the endlessly repeating mantra that she somehow deserved it. This was the key for unlocking the truth of what really happened to her, so she could rearrange the puzzle pieces of her psyche in a new and healthy way. It was her way of declaring "this was not just", rather than believing it was she who misunderstood, that she should be appreciative of her abusers' "love". The intensity of her anger reflected the magnitude of this transformation. It was her body's way of pouring out all the pressure she had held in to continue the illusion that pain was love. The dam was getting ready to break open.

Of course, it was necessary to help Angela channel the anger in appropriate ways. To accomplish this, I needed to have her shift her focus. I explained to her that her wish to kill many anonymous people was actually an expression of how overwhelming the anger felt, how strong her need to get it out of her. Her real task, and the only way she could get true satisfaction, was to "kill" (in her imagination) the perpetrators of her abuse. This was not only a statement about what would make for successful therapy, it was also a buffer against her impulse to hurt others, which was leaking out in subtle ways (for example, biting remarks at work, extreme impatience and irritability, etc.).

The impulse to kill many anonymous people served one further purpose. By keeping these fantasies general and abstract—focused on nameless, faceless "people out there"--she was avoiding the need to confront her abusers. In this way, she was still protecting those whose love she secretly wanted. On the surface, she felt herself getting angry at the injustice she saw in the world and wanted to respond to that. But until she became willing to face the truth about her abusers, she would not be able to recognize that her over-reaction to injustice in the world was based on her childhood history. Therefore, she would never be able to satisfy her anger, no matter how much she raged at the world, for the original source would be left unaddressed.

As Angela came to understand that it was actually her perpetrators she needed to "kill", and that her anger at injustice in general was born out of the injustice she experienced at their hands, she became ready to take the next step in her therapy.

I knew that it was safe to allow Angela's anger to express itself. This is not always the case; some people must be helped to learn healthy controls over such impulses so they do not act out in harmful ways. Angela, however, was just the opposite. Having spent a lifetime suppressing her anger, my job was to evoke it and coax it out of her. This was a major challenge for her, requiring nothing less than the courage to face the very emotions she originally felt the need to split off from.

Angela's line "I am sure that I wanted Todd to fix this problem" confirms the idea that it was safe for me to encourage her anger. Such a confession speaks volumes about who she is and the strategy behind her defense system. It tells us that she split off into multiple personalities as a way to keep from being angry. It also reveals much about the transference she had with me, seeing me as a safety net that made it possible to express her anger without fear. She never really wanted to act on these impulses and I'm quite sure she could never hurt anyone. But her need to fantasize so vividly in this way brought essential relief from her psychological pressure. Notice that her fantasies centered around killing people who reminded her of her past (those who would sleep with her in an abusive way) and situations of injustice (men cheating on their wives). Fantasy is a way to relieve the pressure of unmet needs, and we all engage in it for this purpose. But Angela's fantasy developed into a distinct personality that wanted to do the killing. With this, the experience of believing she could and would kill was more real to her than it might have been to someone else, in that she could enter into that personality's world-view so thoroughly.

Normally, we buffer such feelings with the "reality check" of other aspects of ourselves—often called our conscience. For Angela, this conscience was held by other personalities within, keeping her from acting on her destructive impulses. But because she perceived these personalities as distinct from one another, she would speak from her anger as if it were a complete personality, one that represented all of who she was at that moment. Still, we both knew that she could never really act on these impulses. Despite the intensity of her fantasies, the other personalities were always operating in the background, keeping her functioning in a socially appropriate way.

This also explains the denial that had her believe I would approve her plan of action: not only was she was trying to deny that these other personalities, those which held her conscience, would prevent her from carrying out the fantasies. She was trying to deny that I, too, represented this conscience, this need for reality-orientation, and would certainly not approve. Her need for the relief her fantasies gave her had her fantasize my approval. In the back of her mind, however, she knew that when it came time to put this to the test, I would try to stop her. Again, the overall "Angela" wanted me to stop her. She simply needed the "hope" her fantasies gave her until the time came for action.

To know Angela is to readily understand that her overall personality could never harm others. She is, despite these fantasies, an unusually kind person, and one who has a deep commitment to treating others well. The incident at seventeen where she did try to kill her father was different; any of us can be pushed to the point of killing if the pressure and threat are great enough. And at such a young age, her defense system was still forming. She had not yet developed enough ego strength to stand up to the abuse in a more "adult" way. But as she grew older, the sweetness of the children inside, as well as the strength of the more functional adults within, developed into a woman whose genuine caring and concern for others is, again, rare.

Healing the memory of the animals was about more than resolving a memory of physical abuse. As she catharted the pain of what was done to her, she was cleansing the emotions that went with it. These emotions held the anger that had been erupting at this time in her therapy, anger that she had not been allowed to express at a younger age over what was done to her. The episode had all the more meaning because Angela had always identified with animals, from the time when her dog "Toy" was the only one with whom she could give and receive love. Angela's earlier description of how she comforted and loved her dog when it, too, had been abused reveals her need to empathize with and see herself in another. It was as if she were holding onto a sense of self by loving this dog, holding onto an identity that could live in this reality by virtue of the love she experienced with him. In identifying with animals in general, she was loving something the way she herself wanted to be loved. When she cleaned off the animals in this memory, she was cleaning off the parts of herself that needed to be loved and made innocent again.

Chapter 20

Tang

While all of this was going on, the *little ones* were integrating. It was a slow process which needed support from within the unit as well as from Todd and myself. It started with the *little ones* getting bigger. A personality was born to house the *little ones* while they were on their journey. Her name was *Tang*. She was the vehicle and a safe haven for the *little ones* before they were ready to be fully integrated. I did not knowingly create her but I did name her. The "T" in *Tang* stood for Todd and the "ang" for Angela. She needed a name so Todd could speak to her but she knew she was temporary and therefore did not choose a name for herself. The name I chose was to represent the work that Todd and I were doing together. *Tang's* function was different than the others. She housed all of the personalities as one, yet each kept their individuality at the same time.

Tang was a young adult and took her job very seriously. From the time she came into being, Todd and I ceased making direct contact with any of the *little ones*.

In the beginning, even though *the little ones* were happy to be part of *Tang*, they were worried that Todd would forget them. *Tang* felt their fear and mentioned it to Todd as she always did when there was a problem. Todd's reply did help but they needed more. They needed to know before they

169

became one that they would be remembered and that their pain would not be forgotten. *Tang* came up with the solution. *Tang* spent one whole day getting ready. She went through every drawer and storage place to look for material that *the little ones* could use to make a collage of their faces. All the material was laid out on the table with a pair of scissors, glue, stickers, paper, feathers, and whatever else she could find. One by one *the little ones* spoke to *Tang* telling her how they wanted to be remembered. *Tang* followed their lead. With each one that came forward, he or she brought at least one other who was too fearful to make an image of themselves but still wanted to be part of the project, and most importantly, did not want to be forgotten. They were laid in the collage under the one who was willing to be seen. It was very emotional and many times there were tears. *Tang* helped them make their faces become alive and *Tang* was able to see them for the first time. Some came forward and wanted to show the pain and fear, yet others wanted to show a happy face. A face of the future in some and in others a face of the present. It was a present to Todd. It was their "good-bye and we love you" tribute. Hours later when it was done no one could look at it, not even *Tang*. It was put into a bag to be presented to Todd during the next session. *Tang* could not look at the pain nor could *the little ones.* It was, as planned, given to Todd and he was asked to put it away – and it was never mentioned again until now.

Tang

Todd's commentary

As with everything else in our work together, Angela's remarkable ability to visualize proved a central feature that always helped promote her healing. In this case, she visualized the integration of her personalities as a literal joining of many into one. She further visualized this process as each of the little ones "getting bigger", which meant growing up. The creation of Tang was a masterful invention for coordinating the individual needs of each sub-personality, enabling them to grow up to the point where they could surrender their individuality into the greater whole.

Angela once described this phenomenon by saying Tang had one body, she was one "person", made up of many bodies, which were meshed together. She said, "If you looked closely you could see the "little ones". I remember at one point, when talking to Tang, she said "all their eyes just opened at the same time when you spoke".

With the arrival of Tang, Angela was ready to take an important step toward wholeness; the little ones no longer needed an independent, individuated voice. She could not yet see them as fully joined together, though, in one personality. The combination of joining and independence that Tang represented was a creative compromise for this stage of her development.

Angela's capacity for visualization, and for relating to her visualizations as real, shows up again in her description of Tang's "physical" growth with the integration of the little ones. With this description, she gives us an uncanny insight into the experience of non-integration. To feel "unsecured", as if a continual movement were going on inside of her, is a wonderful depiction of what it must be like not to experience one's wholeness, not to experience the "integrity" of one's component parts that gives a more solid feeling. As she healed, she felt this integrity as a heaviness, something that anchored her to reality. This made it possible for her to withstand the "gusts" of everyday life which formerly threatened to blow her over.

Chapter 21

Shark

The next step for me required going into a closed room deep inside that housed the memories and people from the past that were locked up a long time ago.

To do this, I had to act on my anger. *Tang*, being very passive, was not able to take me into the dark room, so another personality was manifested. *Tang* would wait for the final 1% which would allow her to become totally one inside and then just as totally one with me. This did happen, but not before *Shark* entered the picture.

My anger had a name and it was *Shark*. *Shark* wanted teeth – big teeth that could rip someone's head off. She told Todd that she was the first of three. The other two never did show up as individuals, but the mission *Shark* was on was threefold: anger, forgiveness, and spirituality. *Shark* was filled with anger. *Shark* was anger. *Shark* wanted to kill and maim. She had no guilt or shame for her thoughts and no remorse for the consequences.

Nor did she have a problem telling Todd what her plans were and didn't really want to listen to his response. She was a person of action and Todd, she thought, was all about talk. At first, she didn't want to spend any more time with Todd than necessary. She had a purpose and did not like the thought that

Todd might try to interfere. *Shark* was designed to kill and she was ready to fulfill her duty. She thought Todd was okay but could not understand why she was talking to him. He wanted to soften her, and she wanted to beat him up.

Talk.....that is all Todd wanted to do. Oh this was torture, just sitting and making believe that she was listening to him. *Shark* needed action and finally one day Todd agreed that it was time for *Shark* to use her teeth.

Shark helped me to eat the people from my past.

I have never experienced or had any desire to eat people before or since. It all took place during a time span of two weeks, and I can still remember the feelings that were associated with eating people with my bare hands.

I needed to get my anger out and I knew who was going to be the first, but not only, recipient. I believe we started by Todd telling me to beat them up on a pillow and I said that beating them up was not enough. He suggested that I kill them, in my mind, but even that was not enough. They could rise from the dead. It had to be final. I decided to visualize eating them, or should I say their essence, while they were alive. I would have to go through all of the physical motions to satisfy my needs. It had to feel real. I wanted to see their faces before I ate them. I remember Todd being a little concerned with my request, but he felt that I should try it and any problems would be taken care of.

The first people I ate were people of no importance. They were abusers who were business acquaintances of my father. I didn't know their names and it felt like this is where I should begin. They were all in a room with one door. The door was usually closed but I opened it.

I could see everyone clustered together in the room. They were the past and they were the executioners of the past and I the executioner of the present. They were the ones that hid their secrets behind closed doors. They were the ones that I feared would kill me. I thought they had the power, but now I knew that I was the one with the power. I hid by the door opening. When they came to the door to see why it was opened, I quickly grabbed them. I threw my arms around their necks and dragged them out kicking and screaming. They were used to being in charge and this surprise caused them great fear. I looked into their faces. Their looks of horror were perfect. Their screams didn't bother me and the look of pain in their eyes was enjoyable. I could feel a noise starting in my toes and working itself up through my body and out of my mouth. It wasn't a scream - it lasted too long to be a scream. It wasn't crying - there were no tears. It was like a bubble moving from DEEP INSIDE, expanding and coming out of my body. It was loud and it lasted for a few seconds. With each sound I made, I ate and chewed and swallowed. I pushed their bodies into my mouth with my fingers. I could feel their bodies going down my throat and I knew they were gone and would never return. It felt good but it was not enough. There were more in that room and I had to eat each and every one of them.

This room was a dark place in my mind where I kept the worst memories. It was always locked to keep me safe, but it also kept their secrets safe and that would no longer do. This room was also locked to keep the *little ones* safe from the anger. I was always fearful of getting in touch with my anger and now I knew why. I always knew it was bigger than I was and would not let it out unless I was in a controlled situation. Being with Todd gave me that safe place and knowing that Todd would be there when I need him.

I continued with the eating the following week. This time it was family members that had to be eaten. I knew their names and the faces were familiar. I opened the door and they came over to peek out. That was my opportunity to grab them. And grab them I did. Not one at a time but a bunch of them. Dragging them to my safe place, I started to kill them. I tied them up so they wouldn't move and bit off their heads. I chewed and swallowed and bit off the rest of their bodies. The sound that came out of my mouth was so horrifying that I almost wished I could stop it, but I couldn't. It was the sound of my anger and the anger was the strength I needed to carry out my quest. When I was done I felt tired but good. My throat hurt so much the following day I could hardly speak. I knew I wasn't done and the following week would have to be more of the same.

As I walked down the hall to Todd's office and noticed people coming and going I started to become nervous. I started to think of the horrible noise I was making during my sessions and became worried that I might be scaring innocent people walking by in the hallway. I decided that I was going to hold in my screams. It didn't work.

During my next session I ate my mother and brother. It was a repeat of the other episodes, but in some way it felt different. Something was missing and I wasn't sure what it was. I was sure that in time it would be shown to me. The difference had to do with the absence of the clean feeling, the feeling of completion that I had on previous occasions. More work needed to be done with them. I had to have that feeling of completion or I would never allow myself tell my story to anyone.

It wasn't long before I reached this point with my mother, as you will see. In time, I also came to realize that I no longer needed to think my brother loved me. This gave me the freedom to simply let go of the importance I put on him. Once this need was gone, the healing began. The feeling of completion happened naturally, without my quite realizing it.

This feeling of completion that I was seeking throughout therapy had to do with cutting the thread of guilt (that I was wrong) and fear (that I would be punished), and taking in a clean deep breath. But in order to release myself from these thoughts, I had to fully accept that my memories were real and that I was justified in standing up to the abuse. When I began therapy, I didn't know what to believe about myself. After some time, I did come to believe that I had MPD. I still had strong doubts that anything terrible happened to me to cause me to have MPD.

I had no memory of any abuse and could not accept the fact that there was something terrible in my past. Even after a few years of therapy when the memories started to surface, I still denied the validity of my memories. My argument was that children always told tales and could not be believed. Todd never tried to sway me one way or the other. His comments were always the same: "Let's just work on the fear and the truth will show itself in time." As long as there was one ounce of doubt that what I was remembering was false, I knew I would never tell my story. I would never hurt anyone with lies. As the years went by and my memories became clearer, it was obvious that my memories were true and that blew me away. I had to deal with the hurt. Once the hurt was addressed and I could look my abusers in the face, hypothetically, I knew that I would be able to tell my story.

Telling my story then became a desire to share my healing and to show other people that there are success stories with happy endings.

Todd's commentary

Shark was originally going to be named Storm or Hurricane, with images of lightning and thunder expressing Angela's anger. But then it was decided the name needed more "teeth" so the personality could really bite, chew and, as we have seen, swallow the objects of her anger.

We must not be offended by the violence that Shark represented. The sounds which came out of her were a literal expression of the pain and anger which had been bottled up and split off for so long. Certainly, this is understandable given the torments she was subjected to. So, too, with the apparent violence of wanting to eat people. Biting is a powerful urge we all experience when young and holds a primeval satisfaction for the control it gives. When all other controls are taken away, as in Angela's case, such a release of primitive energies is absolutely necessary for reclaiming one's boundaries. These expressions of anger, therefore, were actually attempts to "make the abuse stop". And this is true about anger in general; it is always an attempt to take care of oneself. Only when it is repressed and the need behind it is not given a chance to be heard is anger dangerous, for then it operates behind the scenes and outside our awareness. Anger that harms is anger that would force others to hear and recognize the need being expressed. In the appropriate context, the healthy expression of anger actually prevents harm and is healing for all involved.

Angela has bravely shown us the anger that is

potential in us all, though our guilt might hide the fact. We must come to terms with all parts of ourselves if we are to harness their energies and make them our own for constructive, socially useful purposes. Otherwise, they inevitably become destructive, if not to others than certainly to ourselves.

This point is so crucial it bears repeating. If we are to heal, we must fearlessly face all truths within ourselves, no matter how unpleasant, no matter how discrepant with what we want to believe about ourselves. For this reason, the gruesomeness of Shark's behavior was unavoidable. She had to find something that was powerful enough to match the intensity and horror of what had happened to her if she were to become free. No sugar-coated forgiveness would work here. As she said, pounding out her anger on a pillow was not enough, nor was simply "killing" them in an ordinary way. The experience of eating, using the full power of the jaw muscles, like an animal grinding its prey with her teeth and then digesting, absorbing, "owning" them in her being, proved to be the necessary way for Angela to release the extraordinary pain and anger held in for a lifetime.

Of course, this kind of work needs to be done in a protected, safe environment. Our pain does not give us license to act out irresponsibly. In no way, however, is this an impediment to a "complete" catharsis and healing. Angela's work took place in a psychologist's office--or better, it took place in her imagination--and still, it held all the power and reality that she needed it to have. After all, our problems are always the result of beliefs we hold about what is happening to us, so healing always takes place in the mind. Once we attach to our beliefs, we project them out onto others and onto the world. Healing is a matter of owning the projections--which can be done perfectly well in a therapy setting--and withdrawing them back into the mind which made them. At that point, we are free to choose a different set of beliefs, one more in accord with truth and one which will make our lives more fulfilling and peaceful.

The fact that Shark had no guilt or shame, no "conscience", once again sheds light on the purpose MPD is designed to serve. One personality can fulfill a function that other aspects of the person would want to interfere with in some way. For example, the fear of the little ones, their need for love, often interfered with Angela's ability to function in daily life. Angela once told me about a time when she, as an adult woman with children, was grocery shopping. She passed by an aisle with children's toys and spontaneously, with no conscious control, picked up a "dolly" which one of the little ones desired. The Boss, therefore, was created to take care of the little ones while Angela went to work and took care of practical tasks.

In this case, Shark was created to express anger without the interference of Angela's guilt, that which caused her to blame herself instead of her abusers, so that she could hold onto the idea that they truly loved her. My initial challenge, in getting Shark to ally with me, was to have her recognize the need to act on this anger in a way that worked, rather than to simply "kill and maim". We had to find a safe and responsible way to meet her need without diluting the intensity of her "bloodlust".

It was fascinating for me to witness two further things: Shark's lack of guilt and shame, and therefore her lack of concern for approval, created a very different feeling in the room from the other personalities. It was strange not to have a sense of connection with her, an emotional tie, such as I had with all the others. She truly didn't care what I thought at first. It was only when I convinced her she couldn't fulfill her mission without my strength, that she wasn't strong enough to carry out her task on her own, that I found an "in" and we became allies. My promise was to help her "grow her teeth" so they would become big enough to do the job.

But here again is an important example of the fact that there was still a certain degree of superego, of conscience, operating while Shark was present. As mentioned before, the other personalities did have a distant influence even though they seemed to be completely out of the picture while Shark was "out front". I knew this because Shark was willing to listen to me say that she couldn't simply kill all those nameless people as she wanted; she wasn't strong enough, she would be stopped by others who were stronger, and they weren't really the people she needed to direct her anger at anyway. It was also knowing this that I was able to face my own fear of encouraging Angela/Shark to unleash her anger, trusting that she would never allow herself to truly hurt anyone; that this was ultimately in the service of her healing and therefore a safe process.

More than that, it was an essential process.

The second point of note is the way in which Angela's face changed—dramatically!—when she became Shark. Her mouth seemed to become much larger and her bottom lip curled down to expose what appeared to be huge teeth. The rest of her face virtually disappeared behind this giant mouth. The degree to which her appearance changed, the reorganization of the musculature in her face and the look in her eyes, was truly uncanny.

It also bears repeating that what we would call Angela's imagination was actually another reality for her--real in every way. In writing her story, she had to struggle a bit with communicating this with the reader, for her way of recounting events sometimes made it sound as if these things were happening in "objective" reality. This is just another testimony to the power of her visualizations, or better, her multi-sensory fantasies which she took to be real.

What Angela didn't say in her recounting was just how difficult it was for her to open the door where these people of the past were living--how brave she had to be to do so, facing her fear with the growing anger and power we had been developing. This was "the door" that had been so tightly closed her entire life. As she was getting ready to approach it, she realized that in fact she was the one who had been keeping it closed, by way of locking her memories in and making herself safe from them. Now, with me right beside her for strength and support, she as

"Shark" would dare to enter.

It was during this time that Angela decided to "tell her story". As she has said, she needed to develop the courage to first believe her memories were real and then look at them without guilt and self-recrimination, before this telling would be possible. Then it became apparent that sharing her story, breaking the promise of silence she had made to her family, would be a necessary part of the healing process. It came to represent a declaration of her freedom from the past and her power to choose her actions, without the guilt and fear that had always held her back.

Our success with this part of the therapy helped me to grow as a therapist, developing even more confidence that the therapeutic process, when the therapist steps aside and "listens", is always safe and has an extraordinary inherent wisdom. I am convinced that anything can be healed if the patient has enough willingness and the therapist adopts this posture.

That Shark could resolve her anger has profound implications for our potential healing as a humanity. The part of Angela's personality that had separated off into Shark was essentially sociopathic--it had no conscience or guilt, no ability to empathize with or relate to another's feelings. This, it may be said, is the underpinning of all our social ills, the domination by those in power who are not empathizing with the needs of others. A true sociopath is not born without this empathic ability. It is, as with Shark, a protective device…like any other defense system. Of course, the consequences can be horrific but the root cause is the same. And therefore it can be worked through like any other defense system. The only requirement is that one has a true willingness to do so, and this willingness can only come when one sees a greater reward in healing than in holding onto the defensive structure. A sociopathic person would have to believe that it was better to join with others than to cut him or herself off from their feelings. They would have to believe that it was important enough to join with others that they were willing to face all the fears that had them cut off their emotional relating in the first place. In the same way, we as a society and world must come to believe that it is better--that it is, in fact, necessary for survival--to join with each other and with our environment than to serve our separate interests.

Shark's healing process provides a magnificent model for this potential. She first had to join with me, believing I could help her to accomplish her goal better than she could alone. Then, she had to be willing to face the feelings which were so abhorrent to her that she had locked them up in a room deep inside. Only *because* she had joined with me could she then make a new personality choice. Instead of the guilt and fear she had been choosing all her life, Angela was able now to respond with the natural anger that had been so long repressed, an anger which had been keeping *her* locked up inside. Once freed from fear and guilt, she no longer needed the anger. The original source of her pain that caused her to react as she did no longer had any charge for her.

She was free to choose her response and, as we shall see, ultimately forgive and "join with" her abusers as well.

Chapter 22

Forgiving My Father And Mother

My father was the last victimizer left in the room. Before we even started the session I knew that I would not eat him. I tried to kill him once when I was seventeen, having held in the anger all the years up until then. When I tried to kill him, that anger had been allowed to come out. My actions and my words that day allowed me to feel a sense of completion. What I needed to do now was to forgive him.

As I entered the room, he was sitting on a chair in the dark and he was alone. I visualized a forgiving light flooding the room he was in and very slowly the light started to change his appearance as well as the room. The light started at his face and grew brighter and larger, extending out around him. The white light began to move like it had a pulse and eventually became two angels, one on each side of him. By now his face was softer. He didn't look mean and angry as I had always remembered him. I was experiencing the same light and feeling its warmth. We were sharing something: Love - the kind of love that doesn't hurt. The angels began to lift him, ascending upward and he actually smiled. I do not believe that I have ever seen my father smile and it was wonderful. He has been dead for many years, but I do feel that my forgiveness in this experience has touched him in the afterlife. I do believe that forgiveness is never wasted.

Even though I had such a wonderful experience forgiving my father, I was still thinking of revenge for the others.

My next experience was with my mother. I had already eaten her, yet as I stated before, it did not seem finished. Todd and I explored a variety of ways to satisfy my need. Nothing seemed quite right, so Todd suggested that we just start somewhere and see what turn of events took place. What followed was probably one of the highest experiences I have had in or out of therapy.

Todd first suggested that I talk to her and tell her how much she hurt me. I visualized her sitting down next to me and then began talking. I told her how much I had always needed her and how she had never been there. I told her that her acknowledgment of my past and the pain it held was what I needed to hear from her. She said nothing. I told her that just hearing "I am sorry" would be enough. She turned away and I looked at Todd through tears and said, "It's not working." Todd told me to tell her what she would gain if she would be honest and truthful about the part she played in my past. So I tried again.

While she was still sitting next to me, I turned from facing Todd to facing her and said, "You always wanted me to love you. I tried but could never fulfill your wish. If you will admit to the truth and say you are sorry for your part, I will guarantee you my love forever." She moved closer to me and a smile appeared where there had been none. I felt a warm presence instead of a cold chill and this time I turned to Todd and said, "It's working." I turned back to face her and continued by telling her that she would be in my heart and gestured by touching my heart with my hand. A moment of silence passed between us and then she spoke for the first time since we sat down together. My mother said, "I am sorry for everything. Please forgive me." I reached over and held her with love. I brought her towards me and placed her in my heart. I felt loved, truly loved and, more astonishing, I also felt loving. I was able to experience loving my mother, a dream I have had all my life. Unlike my father who I sent home with the angels, my mother will always be a part of me because she will always be in my heart.

Todd's commentary

I will always remember the feeling in the room when Angela forgave her father. It was truly a holy experience, one of those rare moments where the world fades from awareness and the intensity of the moment fills one's consciousness completely. There was a stillness and a fullness in this moment that spoke of a higher reality whose presence overwhelmed all other thoughts. I believe this is what creates the feeling of "being humbled" in mystical experience.

With the experience of forgiving her mother, Angela had successfully internalized the ideal of love. She had replaced the concept of a love that was built on fear and pain with the experience of a love that doesn't hurt. She allowed love in for the first time in her life since before she was four years old, making room in her mind for a self-image that was worthy of receiving and giving real nurturing. As she said "I felt loved, truly loved and, more astonishing, I also felt loving". This is what mothers are supposed to be, like a Madonna for the holy child we all know ourselves to be in our souls. Angela's experience with the mother of her imaginary conversation (or perhaps we should say the mother she was conversing with in a spiritual way) was a major step in transforming her guilt and fear, discovering her true nature underneath all the twisted messages that had been forced upon her.

Chapter 23

Taking Stock Of My Life

I will never be the same again. Once I forgave my parents and knew that I was loved, I had no more need of separate personalities. Now the integration was complete.

Before the abuse started I would join the other side of reality whenever I wanted to feel loved. It just seemed to be so natural for me to leave my body for a different world. The other world consisted only of colors and feelings; it was easy to go there for comfort and safety. I believe all children have this ability and most use it often.

When the abuse did start, I automatically went to my other world but was not able to stay or find comfort there. When the pain became too severe, it would bring me back to my body. Something had to be done so I could stay in my other world and not feel the pain. I had to be able to be in two places at the same time. As the pain increased, I held on more tightly to my other world. It was like someone was pulling me by my legs while I was holding on by my hands. Then it happened: the pulling stopped and I was now two people. I didn't really understand what was happening, I just knew that things were different. I was now able to come and go within my two worlds freely. Other personalities were born out of need and necessity. When a personality that was already established could not take any more abuse, the pull would start again. Each time this happened the process became easier and the time it took became shorter. One personality did not make another one except in the case of the adults. The *little ones* existed totally within themselves. They had an invisible string that attached them to each other. A bond, a silent voice that only they could hear. The other personalities might look after the *little ones* but could never get close. Not until Todd came along did anyone ever speak to them as individuals.

I remember, as a child, a picture hanging in my bedroom of a Guardian Angel watching over two children crossing a bridge. Going into that picture was something I did often. It was my hiding place. I sat there until it was safe to return, and I brought my brother with me. When we moved my mother left the picture and I was heartbroken. My mother had no idea what the picture meant to me and I never told her. I still miss it and think of it often.

Personalities like Tang, the Boss, and Shark came into being differently. Unlike the children, they were not born out of pain and fear. They came into being because of a need that had to be met. The need was not known to me but was known to all inside. When a personality was needed to be an adult, the inner force created by the ones inside would cause me to step aside once again. Their needs created the personality. Stepping aside became something I did willingly and without much convincing from the ones inside.

I was now ready to start my new life. I felt healed and was not afraid of the past any longer. I felt loved and was starting to love myself as well. What could be better, what more could I ask for, how could I not be absolutely perfectly happy?

Todd's commentary

It is said that we create our reality and I take this to be literally true. We can only know reality by our perception of it, and our perception of it, I believe, is completely determined by the psychological choices we make. We cannot make direct contact with an objective reality "out there" but only with our interpretation of it, filtered through our senses. Again, this interpretation is completely determined by our psychological make-up.

So when Angela describes in the remarkable passage above how her MPD first developed, she is describing the way she transformed her perception of reality by choosing a different interpretation of what was going on for her. The need to create a different interpretation had become an imperative; she absolutely "had to be in two places at once". And so she found a way to allow her body to remain in physical reality while she perceived a different reality. This different reality and the personality she created that lived in it, were the product of internal choices that were adaptive to her need.

In fact, we all do this all the time, choosing to attend to certain aspects of reality while filtering out others, according to our preferences and needs. Personality is a byproduct, we might say, of these choices, the result of our chosen perceptions about who we are, what reality is and how to respond to it--again, according to adaptive need.

My 5 year-old daughter recently demonstrated this in a most interesting way. As she learns to sublimate her aggression--understanding that it is not permissible to express it in hurtful ways but also understanding that she is entitled to have her feelings--she is trying out different approaches to achieving this balance. At one point she was quite angry about not getting her way and was busy being defiant like any 5 year old. At the next moment, her mother asked "What are you angry about?", and she replied, "I'm not angry. So-and-so is angry!" This so-and-so (I don't remember the name) was a made up "personality", projected out as a "real" person in reality, that allowed her to displace her anger so she did not have to take responsibility for it. This is precisely the same thing that Angela has described above and, again, is something we all do in subtle ways often. Only the degree to which someone with MPD does this determines the difference.

Consider the effect when a policeman puts on his uniform and suddenly "becomes" a policeman. He then goes home after work and starts playing with his child and an entirely different personality comes out. Doctors may wear their title as a badge of authority that too often separates them from their patients. When they become the patient, their perspective can shift dramatically. Our job, then, is to understand the hidden motives behind the many "personalities" we all choose at different times, and then learn to express ourselves directly, without fear and defensiveness. We want to be our true selves in every situation. Ultimately, we want to own all parts of ourselves, integrating them into one, to most effectively deal with whatever circumstance comes our way, and live our lives fully expressed, potential fulfilled and inner peace realized.

Chapter 24

Integration A Whole New Meaning:

The Book Of Life

At first I was very happy indeed. I felt free from all the chains of shame I had carried around with me all of my life. Then one average day at work a problem popped up, and I started to panic. A rude awakening was about to be thrust upon me and I was not prepared. In the past I could always split off when things began to overwhelm me but now I literally stood alone. The first problem at work was taken care of, a second incident was handled as well, but by the third event, I was losing my confidence and felt that I was now part of a world different from anything else I had experienced. What would have seemed like everyday problems to others were big problems for me. I felt so alone. I waited patiently to talk to Todd.

I had had a plan; I would do what would be necessary to be healed. I made a promise to the *little ones* that I would take care of them. What I neglected to plan was "the rest of my life". For years I thought of nothing else but becoming "one" and just assumed that I would live happily ever after. Todd told me on many incidents that once there we would continue to work on living in the "regular world." I ignored him; I wasn't going to have any problems in the "regular world".

But now that I had healed my past, it was time to heal the present. I was devastated. Looking at my life I could see a void of love. I wasn't done my work and all of a sudden felt very tired. Todd came to my rescue and said, "As we did in the past, so shall we do it now, one day at a time." I cried. I was not looking at the big picture when it came to being healed. One night just before I fell asleep, I felt pushed to go to my computer and type. The result was an explanation on healing by Angel. I have shared that with you in the appendix.

At the beginning of my therapy, I mentioned a dream where my guide said that he would return once I was done with my journey to oneness. As he promised, he did return, and came to help me re-write the Book of Life. A book where we make the major decisions that alter our lives. A book that allows us to "change our minds" and therefore change our lives.

The work I needed to do concerning the Book of Life had to do with the next step in my integration process. I had already integrated within myself and now it was time to integrate with the world. This meant allowing love to enter my life and also allowing love to flow out and touch others. I had no idea how scary that would be until we started the actual work. I felt such a resistance and couldn't explain why. It felt like I was facing walls that were tall, strong and had existed for many years. We would take what Todd called "baby steps" so as not to scare me away. One step forward and sometimes one or two steps back. This went on for months. I thought I had faced it all and truly did not expect this to happen. It sounded so easy, yet it literally took my breath away. And then I saw it: as I was trying to explain how I was feeling, a picture appeared just to the right of Todd. It was a large book with writing on it that was too blurred to read. Yet I knew it was important and also knew that I had to stay with it until the mystery of it was solved. Todd agreed. As the weeks went by, the writing became clearer and the feeling behind the writing was also being shared with me. It was almost a month before the memory came to the surface.

The first thing that happened was I was able to read what was written in the book. It said, *"Shall not let love in nor let love out for eternity"*. Now I knew what was written and soon after it was shown to me what happened that caused it to be written:

I was around ten years old and still had hope that my family would love me once I proved myself worthy. On a daily basis I watched how my mother loved my brother. She hugged him and kissed him tenderly on the cheek. She would continually tell me how wonderful he was and how all of his problems were never his fault. She loved him unconditionally and I wanted the same from her. I could see and hear it but never was allowed to feel it. The "it " was love and up until this day I yearn for it.

The memory continued: I was in my bedroom and my mother and brother were in the kitchen. My mother was giving my brother a talk that I called the "You are wonderful" talk. I decided to go into the kitchen and ask for a "You are wonderful" talk just for me. When I approached them it was as if I was invisible but that didn't stop me. I had been good for years and did just what everyone wanted me to do and now it was my turn. I walked between them and faced my mother whispering "Don't you love me, too?" Her answer was sharp and cruel; "Your brother needs all of my love and all of your love. How can you be so selfish? When are you going to learn that his happiness is all that matters? You are so spoiled. Now apologize to him and tell him how much you love him".

I did as I was told. I told my brother how much he was loved and wanted to know if I could make him feel better. I had done it so many times in the past that this was not new nor was it hard. He punched me and told me to go back to my room and stay out of the kitchen. Walking back to my bedroom defeated changed my whole life.

I closed the door and laid on my bed as I had done so many times before. I allowed myself to drift to a place that no one else could go to. And that is where I made a promise to myself that I have kept for over 50 years. The promise was simple; I was not going to allow myself to be hurt again. I was not going to expect more than what I got. I was going to live without love. My heart would be safely tucked away for the rest of my life. And when I was done, it felt good. I was freed at last from the wanting. And that, as written in the Book of Life, was my turning point.

Todd's commentary

As Angela has said, the first half of our work was about integration of the separate personalities into a single, functioning whole. The second half would now have to be devoted to living in the world in this integrated way: what I called integrating with the world. Angela's defense of splitting off to deal with life's difficulties was no longer viable, and she had no experience in using the regular defenses that most people use. Our work would now be about developing her resiliency, her ability to handle the normal problems of life in a normal way. True integration would mean knowing herself as a whole, "solid" person who could stand up to such problems and not "dis-integrate" in the face of them. It would mean integrating the realities "out there" and coming to peace with them, making them part of her being. Ultimately, it would mean feeling herself to be fully part of the world, expanding her personality to make room for all aspects of life, no longer needing to defend against them.

The greatest challenge of all is to integrate with those "aspects of life" called other people. The fully realized human being is one who has worked through their resistance to any person or situation so that their peace cannot be disturbed. In the end, our goal is to be so secure, so free of fear and defensiveness, so accepting of what is, that we may include *all* people in our world, and do so with love. For where there is no need to defend, love, compassion and understanding are the inevitable result. Without fear, we are no longer bound to think first of ourselves and our personal needs; we are free to *truly* see others' needs. We understand when their actions arise from fear and defensiveness and our only wish is to help them become free as we have become free. This is the highest purpose of integration, a "spiritual" purpose, and represents the farthest reach of human development.

Let us see what happens next as Angela works through the struggle with this stage of her path.

Chapter 25

Letting Love In And Out

I thought that once I was integrated my problems would be over and my new life would immediately start. I was wrong. For one year I continued to struggle with fitting into my new world. Something was missing and Todd said the something was love. Letting love in and out was my new battleground and let me tell you that this soldier was ready to desert. "How could I ever trust anyone enough to love?", I remember saying. There was no memory of love in my past to fall back on or to use as a reference, so I felt helpless. Todd and I continued to work on just this one and last hurdle.

I wanted to remember love but it seemed like I was struggling for something that might not have ever existed. Todd never gave up hope and I never had any. Without love I was nothing and had no value and this nothingness grew as the work intensified. Living without love seemed logical and all I wanted to do was stop looking. I quit, stomped my feet, yelled, and threatened never to talk to Todd again if he didn't let go of this impossible task.

Todd suggested that I visualize my parents standing before me and to ask about their love for me to see if it was there in hiding. I did try and found both of them showed no interest in my quest. They stood before me with their backs turned in my direction. There was a box holding a gift of light just for me but they stood in front of it. I spoke to them and let them know how much their love meant to me and how I was suffering. They just didn't care. Towards the end of the session they did part so I could reach the box if I wanted to, but I didn't want to. I wanted them to give it to me, and even more, give it to me lovingly.

The following session I reluctantly tried again. The second time was like the first with a few changes. They turned around to face me and did offer me the gift of light but not with open arms. It remained on the floor and I again had to retrieve it if I wanted it. I mentally pulled away and spoke to Todd. I told him that it wasn't working and maybe the love just wasn't there. I cried and felt so empty and alone. Todd encouraged me to try one more time and I did.

The third time was different. I approached them not as an adult but as their child. The child before the abuse started. A small voice was heard asking mommy and daddy to love her. A voice that was non-threatening. A miracle happened as they opened up their arms and welcomed me into their love. The box was opened and the light of love surrounded us. The light joined us, not in form but in spirit. It was wonderful. I was around three or four years old and they held me and kissed my cheeks with tenderness.

And then it happened. I found love.

There, in the life of this child, was the love that I was looking for. It was safely tucked away all of this time until I was ready. A memory of love not hurting, of being hugged and protected, and peaceful sleeps. It all came back and filled the empty space with all the good feeling that allowed me to say, "I was loved". My parents loved me before their love was spoiled and that love was enough. Now I could forgive and let go. The feeling of guilt and fear gave way to a new feeling: I mattered. I had been loved once and knew that I could be loved again. Somebody had loved me; that was all I needed to know. I was complete.

The following days consisted of remembering their love and wanting to share it with everyone. I found myself forgiving small injustices which would have normally made me angry. Touching people when I spoke to them, calling people I hadn't talked to in some time, reaching out to be friendly, and not being annoyed at traffic or long lines in the supermarket.

Since then I have had days where the love was forgotten and my old ways returned, but all it took was to be reminded that I was indeed loved and all was well again. All of these years living without love created habits that are hard to break. With Todd's help I am reminded often until the feeling of being loved becomes the new habit.

The line in the Book of Life has faded in time and is now ready to be re-written. It is being re-written as I write this and will continue to do so. As one line fades, another line replaces it immediately. This is one of the rules of the Mind and is what allows us to make changes in either direction. We can move closer to our spiritual self--love--or go in the opposite direction--fear--at any given time. So now it is time to restore the Book of Life to its original state. As I do so, I am able to watch the new words, and even the page number, begin to appear, and I sit in awe.

Page 1134 now reads: I am loved and therefore will love for eternity.

Each page following this page changes as well, right up to today. What was in the past is now looked upon with different eyes. The effect that page 1134 has on the remaining pages is astronomical. Each page builds on the other and I am now in the process of building a new life.

Todd's commentary

Angela is indeed becoming free to rewrite the Book of Life in a new and joyous way. Her remarkable work has released her from the prison of the past to be able to choose her future and to choose the life *she* wants to create. As I watch her continue to grow, I take immense pride and pleasure in seeing her learning to love others, letting others love her, and expanding her integration to include more and more of life's adventure. She is becoming less afraid of embracing challenge, taking risks, interacting with people and situations that broaden her world far beyond the tiny confines of her previous existence. With this, she expresses her freedom from the past by wanting to help others discover these same possibilities for themselves, a wish and a need which led to the writing of this book. It is my hope as well that this story may inspire those who read it to reach for their own integration, that it may promote the release from suffering and further the goal of our collective wholeness.

Epilogue

Facing our fears and relinquishing our defenses opens the door to healing and wholeness. It allows us to find our truth and write a new story for our lives once love settles in. In her therapy, Angela had to face her fear of accepting the truth about her family, letting go the fantasy of love, and setting herself free from a lifetime of isolation and self-blame. Blaming herself was her chief defense against blaming her family, and only the realization that she could afford to and indeed had to confront them would release her. With this, she was able to integrate the truth about who she was. She no longer needed the separate personalities to defend against the abuses that threatened her fantasy of love. This cleared the way for her to let the real meaning of love come through.

We cannot escape the prospect of getting wounded. It seems we enter into this life ready to become afraid. The fact that life brings constant change means we are constantly confronted with threats to our identity, and preserving our identity can be even more important to us than preserving our lives. When a threat to our identity comes along, we cling desperately to what we have known, sometimes preferring the loss of all hope over change. We reach for any means possible to hold onto how we believe things must be for us to feel safe and whole. Angela's way of coping with the extraordinary threats which confronted her was to make a sub-identity for each new challenge. In this way, she could protect her core identity, her original idea of being part of a loving family. Of course, this was necessary for her survival, the best she could do as a young child. But as she matured in therapy, she developed the tools and resources for handling these threats in a new way. Unlike the child, she could now choose a more effective response, one built on a solid self-esteem and a newfound feeling of safety and love.

This, then, is the secret to healthy childhood development, or to healing the wounded child within us, and nurturing a new generation of healthy adults. We must help the "child", whenever they feel threatened, to discover that they, too, can deal effectively with their situations rather than defending against them. With this, they come to know the world as manageable, navigable and ultimately friendly.

As we raise our children this way, or tend our own childhood wounds, they and we learn to adapt creatively to whatever life may bring. Instead of spending our lives building and fortifying walls of protection, seeing ourselves at war with the world, we may be encouraged to embrace change as an invitation to expand and grow. Rather than meeting new situations as potential challenges to our integrity, to be defended against at all costs, we may understand our response to them as reflecting something in our psyche, just as Angela did. Thus, problems become lessons in how to reach fulfillment, and obstacles become opportunities to soak up the variety of experiences life can bring, treasure chests to be opened, revealing the gold of who we truly are.

The fundamental problem in being human is this: we go into battle with reality when it conflicts with the way we wish things to be. We dissociate ourselves from what would require too drastic a change in our identity and insist that the situation conform to our wishes. This is the cause of all relationship struggles, holy wars, political rebellions and environmental problems. Our human nature would have us attempt to force the world, especially other people, to change so that *we* do not have to. Of course, the world does not comply.

Integration and healing are matters of recognizing this fact; they come as we realize that life is not to be lived in the endless pursuit of satisfying our wishes and avoiding our fears, insisting that the world meet our needs. Even when presented with the kind of difficulties Angela had to face, it is necessary, whether we like it or not, that we work *with*, not against, our problems. We must reach with all of our courage for a better solution, rather than demanding the problems "go away", dissociating from them in some way to imagine they have disappeared. This only magnifies the problems, as we see in the present global crisis, for the fear at their core is left unaddressed, wreaking havoc in the unconscious of the world.

We must give up our place at the center of our world-view. To dance gracefully with life and all of its change, we must stop relating what happens to us according to how well it does or does not promote our personal wishes. The circumstances of our lives and the affairs of the universe are simply not designed to serve our self-interested concerns. The great goal of spiritual maturity is to learn to allow reality to be what it is, without imposing our fantasies and demands upon it. We want to practice framing our response to human affairs in the light of what will serve the higher good, what will promote workability in our world, and what will further the cause of greater harmony for humankind. This is the larger goal of psychotherapy and spiritual growth.

The full spiritual potential of integration has us naturally transfer our pre-occupation with self to a compassionate interest in others. The fear that drives us to focus too intently on our personal wishes has spawned a world-wide epidemic of defensiveness and aggression. As we give up our self-interested fixations, we quietly embrace the changes of life, and find an Identity that is changeless behind the scenes of all the flux that surrounds us. We are no longer compelled to see ourselves at odds with the rest of the world, but can consider the needs of others and the world as equal to our own. With this, we assume our role as agents in the cause of healing, this becoming the meaning and purpose of our lives.

Integration, then, is more than a psychological endeavor. It must be the goal of our highest spiritual aspirations. Ultimately, full integration brings insight into what we have been defending against not only in our personal histories, but what aspects of the nature of reality, of the questions of life and death and of the human spiritual experience we have been refusing to address. Even more importantly, we gain insight into why and how our denial occurred in the first place, separating us from the spiritual wholeness we knew before our personal histories began. This kind of insight makes it possible to see through the entire illusion of fear and return to our original innocence.

As we free ourselves from fear, integration moves beyond the concerns of the individual to become a group matter. Just as Angela integrated the separated parts of herself into a well-functioning whole, she then moved on to integrating her individual self with a larger "Self", one that encompassed the world of other people. What is true for the individual is true for our species; we must know ourselves to be one person, integrating our fractured world into a single functioning whole. In sharing her story, Angela has expressed her need to help others heal as she has been healed, seeing herself in them, recognizing the oneness we all share. Resolving one's personal needs with integration, then, becomes a spiritual gift to the world, helping forward the journey to wholeness for us all.

Again, in moving beyond the personal process of our own integration, we understand the need to participate in the world's integration. Thinking along the lines of what best serves the whole, whether speaking of families, workplaces, neighborhoods, nations or the planet, we must come out of our collective denial if we are to heal our problems. We must resolve our mass dissociation, working through our fears and finding new ways to deal effectively with the challenges of living harmoniously in the world. And finally, we must see ourselves in the bigger picture of who we are as a humanity, that we may mature past the preoccupation with self, to express what is highest and finest in us.

Inevitably, we are all coming to full integration as we learn that fear's ways do not make us safe and can never bring fulfillment. Giving up fear as a tool for "survival", we restore the disowned parts of ourselves to their rightful place, and then restore ourselves to our rightful place in the world. We join with, rather than defend against, that which was previously deemed a threat to our identity, and emerge into a new identity as part of the whole, one with the rest of humankind, and participants in the overall advance of the world. With this, we are truly set free, for nothing forces us into defensive and limiting ways of being, and we do indeed find ourselves in a friendly universe. Our only need then is to share our freedom, expressing ourselves creatively in this wonderful playground of human possibilities. This is the promise of integration and the discovery of wholeness.

In Appreciation

The wisdom teachings of many traditions tell us nothing that happens to us is accidental or without intent. Indeed, we are told our life's journey is designed, if you will, to help us grow into our full potential. After these many years of working with Angela, it is clear to me that the circumstances of her life--from the descent into her abusive childhood, to the burying of these painful experiences in a way that allowed her to function, and then to the therapeutic adventure we undertook together--were no accident. Time and again I was struck with the profound sense of a higher hand at work in shaping our therapeutic progress. It became clear that our work together was meant not only to relieve the pain of her past but to use that past for spiritual growth, the realization of an individual and collective wholeness. I firmly believe we can all expect this kind of realization in our own life journeys, that there are no accidents in the plan for our "homecoming", and that everything that happens to us happens for our ultimate good. Of course, it is difficult if not impossible to see this at times of crisis. But Angela's story, with all of its pain and struggle, clearly demonstrates that the situations of our lives can become a launching pad for our growth. The end goal of this growth is the discovery of our true selves, vastly expanded beyond the limits of the body and our personal history. With this, we spontaneously open to an appreciation of the inherently joyful nature of life.

On a personal note, I must give testimony to my own experience of this idea of "no accidents". For it is very apparent to me that my meeting Angela was "appointed" for my own growth as well. The sense of purpose, fulfillment and higher understanding I have been given through our work has been deeply meaningful for me. I would like to take this opportunity to express my appreciation and to say how privileged I feel to have shared in this experience, how truly grateful for the lessons that were clearly meant for me in our coming together. And last but certainly not least, I want to thank Angela for the chance to walk this journey with her and for the extraordinary person she is.

Appendix

A Note From Angela

At the time of this writing, I had identified the voice in the following passage as Angel, my seeker. As I grew spiritually, so did my acceptance of a power greater than mine. Over time I came to understand Angel as not one of the personalities, but a true spiritual guide. She was with me since birth and did not integrate into "me" with the rest, but remains a presence that is "separate" and distinct from me while still very much connected with me.

If you recall, I said that the Voice in my dreams told me it would not return until my therapy with Todd was complete. In fact, It did return and I now know that this presence is one and the same as what I was calling Angel, as well as the one giving the "magical kiss".

My contact with this presence has been extremely meaningful for me, and continues to this day. Here is one of the writings I received on Healing, which I would like to share with you. If the spiritual tone of the language is not something you can relate to, please feel free to re-interpret it in a way that makes sense to you. As I said, my acceptance of these things has been a natural outgrowth of my own journey, and for me, there is no doubt that such a spiritual reality exists.

Healing

Healing is the melding of the inside (Mind) with the outside (physical reality). It is the combination of what we will call "Level One" and "Level Two", Level One being the physical reality and Level Two the Mind. Healing occurs when the body and the Mind are working as one unit, where the passage of Information is not blocked by bone or matter.

How does healing happen? There is only one step but it takes many small movements to make up that one step. The first movement is to slowly let the light into the darkness, light being Information and darkness being fear or ignorance of the light. Read, listen, open your mind to new thoughts and welcome a higher Presence into your life. Refuse to be ignorant and closed-minded. Acknowledge the ego and take away its power over you with the truth.

Each time you look for the truth, you permit light to shine in the innermost and darkest corners of your mind. Once the smallest amount of light is allowed to shine on the darkness, the healing starts. The willingness to accept change automatically puts you in a state of healing. It cannot be stressed enough that information is the key to healing. Look at your life not through the eyes of the past but the eyes of the future, or even better, the eyes of what can be. Hope and faith mixed with seeking the truth will be the right combination for success. Hope is telling you that you deserve only the best and the best is out there for you to take. Faith takes away all doubt.

The movement is slow. Not because it has to be slow but because you are unable to see the truth all at once. Pick up a piece of your fear and hold it in your hand to review. Turn it around until you see all sides and when the time is right, replace it with the truth. It may physically or mentally hurt because it is hard to let go. How do you replace it? Not alone. It takes three - you, a trust in a higher Presence, and your therapist. Each piece is to be examined and once one piece is healed, move on to the next piece and do the same. Do not let one piece go until it has transformed into light.

Imagine yourself doing this now. Think of something that is preventing you from feeling loved. A person, a situation, a lack of something, or a fear of the future. One thing at a time. It doesn't matter which one; just start. Hold it in your hand and start the process. Remember to bring truth and honesty into the equation. Refuse to let the ego rule. Faith and trust in your therapist are essential and a therapist that agrees with this process is also necessary. Let him or her know that you want to find the truth and replace it with the inner light that each of us have. No one is omitted from this gift and this gift is God's love--remembered.

I will walk you through the healing process that was associated with the multiple personalities. It is the same in every situation--healing one fear at a time. For Angela, it started with the relationship between the patient and the therapist. A bond had to take place that would allow their love to overcome any fear that would arise in the sessions. Once that was established, I entered the picture. Not that I wasn't always there, I just stayed in the background guiding but not making myself known. A silent partner. I gave encouragement and guidance but never took the lead. It is not my way. One by one, the little ones were brought to me for healing. The determination and love between Angela and Todd for the little ones made my job easy. They were looked at from all sides until the fear became love and I was able to take them home. Home in this case is the Mind, which belongs to Me.

The little ones lived in darkness and the ego was determined to keep them there. This would assure the ego that it would not "lose" Angela to the light. Fear to the ego is like truth to the Spirit, bringing you closer to the source. Fear can be attached to anything. You can overcome fear in one situation only to have it attach to another situation. It will continue until you have uncovered all the dark corners one by one and brought each of them to Me.

How does one take care of the obstacles that stand in the way of healing? Once one is healed the obstacles are seen as illusions, yet to heal, they must be dealt with and eliminated as if real. To go from Level One to Level Two we must tag the obstacles for reference. Even though they are equal in the eyes of the Spirit, we see them by degrees of difficulty. Therefore, a decision must be made. First, you have to pick a problem to tackle. It doesn't matter which; just pick one. Let's heal loneliness. It may be your hardest or your easiest problem, depending on all the other factors in your life. I am picking loneliness because people are designed to be lonely. Everyone has experienced this emotion.

From the time of birth to the time of death--we are lonely. Remember I said that information is the key to our spiritual path. Therefore, I want to pass this information on to you and hope you take it as your own. You are lonely because you miss God. Missing your husband that died or missing a friend who has left you is only a memory of the loneliness you feel for God. It reminds you that you are not with the one you truly love. Substitutes help fill the loneliness but are not made to last and they don't. How do you stop loneliness? By being true to yourself. How is that done? By standing nose to nose with the ego and challenging it to a game of truth or dare.

Truth is the strongest weapon anyone has against the ego and even though you can do it alone, I would suggest having help. Fear seems so much stronger and bigger than truth and loneliness is all wrapped up in fear. There is an old saying that goes "Look fear square in the face". That is how the game of truth and dare is played.

First admit that you are lonely. By admitting it, you are encouraging truth to be dominant. Second, admit it to someone else. I would prefer a therapist but a good strong friend would also do. Wait until the uncomfortable feeling leaves you after admitting that you are lonely. How long this takes will depend on how sincere your statement is and how "loudly" you are willing to speak it.

Fear in this case will show up as all the embarrassment that will be attached to this exercise. And fear is put there by the ego. Repeat that you are lonely as often and as loudly as you can. Yelling would even be better. The ego hates the force created by yelling. Once you get used to that, start adding that you are lonely because you miss God

The ego will start fighting back. Don't give up. Continue to seek the truth and you will conquer the ego. Both cannot exist in the same time frame at the same time. Shifting between the Spirit and the ego is common practice at first and most acceptable. It is the shifting between Level One and Level Two. I repeat, don't give up. The more knowledgeable you become, the stronger you become. Be a seeker.

Let me give you an example of how the truth conquers fear and how fear is an illusion.

Where the sky meets the sea seems like an end but is not, for the sky and the sea only give that illusion. Our knowledge of that takes away the fear of going over the edge. Just like the sky and the sea, everything we see is an illusion and knowledge will take away the fear because nothing is as it seems. Before they knew better, people truly believed they would fall off the end of the earth. Think about all the times you thought something similar. "If I face this person, or let myself believe this thought, I will fall to eternity." The truth would let you see that an illusion cannot hurt you.

When people believed that the world was flat, it prevented them from venturing outside of their belief system. Just as they believed that they would indeed fall off the end of the earth, we believe our fear is real. There was no doubt in their minds that what they feared was real, yet you now know it was not true.

It is the same with God. You believe that God punishes and even cries for you. I say it is an illusion. God only knows love. God is love. And where there is love, there is nothing else.

Bibliography

Banathy, B.H. (1973). *Developing a systems view of education: The systems- model approach.* Seaside, CA: Intersystems.

Barach, P. (2000). Guidelines for treating Dissociative Identity Disorder (Multiple Personality Disorder) in adults, *Journal of Trauma and Dissociation,* 1(1), 115-134.

Casey, J. (1992). *Flock: The autobiography of a multiple personality.* New York: Ballantine Books.

Chase, T. (1987). *When rabbit howls.* New York: Jove Books.

Checkland, P.B. (1981). *Systems thinking, systems practice.* Chichester, England: Wiley.

Elkins, D.N., Hedstrom, L.J., Hughes, L.L., Leaf, J.A., & Saunders, C. (1988). Toward a humanistic-phenomenological spirituality: Definition, description, and measurement.
Journal of Humanistic Psychology, 28(4), 5-18.

Frank, J.D. (1961). *Persuasion and healing.* Baltimore, MD: Johns Hopkins University Press.

Gold, S., Elhai, J., Rea, B., & Weiss, D. (2001). Contextual treatment of Dissociative Identity Disorder: Three case studies. *Journal of Trauma and Dissociation,* 2(4), 5-36.

Grof, S. (1980). *Beyond the brain: Birth, death and transcendence in Psychotherapy.* New York: State University of New York Press.

Grof, S. (1988). *The adventure of self-discovery: Dimensions of consciousness and new perspectives in psychotherapy and inner exploration.* Albany: State University of New York Press.

Grof, S., & Halifax, J. (1977). *The human encounter with death.* New York: Dutton.

James, W. (1982). *The varieties of religious experience.* New York: Viking Penguin. (Original work published in 1902).

Keyes, D. (1995). *The minds of Billy Milligan.* New York: Bantam.

Kluft, R.P. (1995). Current controversies surrounding dissociative identity disorder. In L.Cohen, J.Berzoff, & M.Elin (Eds.), *Dissociative Identity Disorder: Theoretical and Treatment Controversies* (pp. 347-377). Northvale, New Jersey: Jason Aronson.

Lowen, A. (1967). *The betrayal of the body.* New York: Harper & Row.

Miller, S.D., & Triggiano, P.J. (1992). The psychophysiological investigation of multiple personality disorder: review and update. *American Journal of Clinical Hypnosis, 35*(1), 47-61.

Moody R. (1975). *Life after life.* Atlanta, GA: Mockingbird Books.

Olson, S. (1997). *Becoming one: A story of triumph over multiple personality disorder.* Pasadena, California: Trilogy Books.

Otto, R. (1958). *The idea of the holy: An inquiry into the non-rational factor in the idea of the divine and its relation to the rational.* London: Oxford University Press. (Original work published in 1917).

Pressman, T. (1999). *Radical Joy: Awakening your potential for true fulfillment.* New York: Kensington Books.

Pressman, T. (1992). The therapeutic potential of non-ordinary states of consciousness as explored in the work of Stanislav Grof. *Journal of Humanistic Psychology, 32*(3), 8-24.

Rank, O. (1952). *The trauma of birth.* New York: Robert Brunner. (Original work published in 1923)

Reich, W. (1949). *Character analysis.* New York: Farrar, Straus & Giroux.

Ring, K. (1980). *Life at death.* New York: Coward, McCann & Geoghegan.

Rossi, E.L. (1986) Altered states of consciousness in everyday life: The ultradian rhythms. In B.B. Wolman & M. Ullman (Eds.), *Handbook of states of consciousness* (pp. 97-132). New York: Van Nostrand Reinhold.

Sizemore, C. (1989). *A mind of my own.* New York: William Morrow.

Sizemore, C. (1978). *I'm Eve.* New York: Berkley Publishing Group.

Smith, C. (1998). *Magic Castle: A mother's harrowing true story of her adoptive son's multiple personalities—and the triumph of healing.* New York: St. Martin's Press.

Spanos, N. (1996). *Multiple identities and false memories: A socio-cognitive perspective.* Washington, D.C.: American Psychological Association.

Thomas, A. (2001). Factitious and Malingered Dissociative Identity Disorder: Clinical Features Observed in 18 Cases. *Journal of Trauma and Dissociation, 2*(4), 59-78.

West, C. (1999). *First person plural: My life as a multiple.* New York: Hyperion.

Wulff, D. (1991). *Psychology of religion: Classic and contemporary views.* New York: Wiley.

Todd E. Pressman, Ph.D. is a licensed psychologist as well as an international lecturer and workshop leader. He has been widely recognized for his work with *A course in miracles* and Transpersonal Breathwork. His book *Radical Joy: Awakening Your Potential for True Fulfillment* has also received high acclaim.

Dr. Pressman has traveled the world to study the great Wisdom and healing traditions. In 1982, he spent time with a Zen master in a monastery in Kyoto, stayed with a Jain family whose reverence for life had them put out sugar each night to feed the ants, met and exchanged with one of only eight remaining Zoroastrian high priests outside the Fire Temples of Bombay, and witnessed authentic fire walking and other fakir ceremonies in Sri Lanka.

His education also includes an internship in Gestalt therapy at the Esalen Institute and training under Stanislav Grof, M.D. in the Spiritual Emergency Network. With a background deeply rooted in tradition (he was trained by a father whose teachers were taught by Sigmund Freud), he has integrated this wide-ranging experience into a new program of psycho-spiritual development. His working model is based on Michelangelo's ideal: to release the statue from the stone, the high spiritual Self from the overlays of imposed identity, into the discovery of true freedom, joy and fulfillment.

He can be contacted at:

The Greens of Laurel Oak
1202 Laurel Oak Road – Suite 207
Voorhees, NJ 08043

Phone: 856-435-1955

www.pressmanandassociates.com

toddpressman@comcast.net

Angela Fisher was born and raised in Brooklyn, New York to first generation Italians. Her childhood was extremely abusive and out of that pain she developed MPD (Multiple Personality Disorder). By the time she was four her first personality in a series of many came to life.

While growing up, the only friend that she had was her inner Guide. He would show her love where none existed otherwise. He stayed with Angela throughout her childhood and still remains active in her life to this day. Once Angela successfully integrated her personalities, she was able to channel her Guide to help others with their spiritual paths as well as their life purposes.

Angela married, went to college, and had two children before she decided to look at her MPD. Only with the help of her therapist, Todd Pressman Ph.D. was she able to face the memories. After the therapy was completed, they decided to co-author *"The Bicycle Repair Shop"*, describing their experiences of her journey and the process required to heal a split mind.

Her passion for painting has brought her beauty and

love in childhood as well as in the present. She is trained in Reiki and Therapeutic Touch and uses them both in combination with her channeling. In addition, Angela volunteers her time in her community to help children and adults needing a friend. She is currently an active student and facilitator of *"A Course in Miracles"*.

My main goal", says Angela, "is to take this freedom from fear and teach others that they too can achieve a life without pain".

She can be contacted at aftang2005@yahoo.com

Printed in Great Britain
by Amazon